"Isaiah 55:8 says that God's thoughts and God's ways are not ours. Kim Patterson's book shares with us her discovery of God's spiritual life, what she learned firsthand, and how it changed her life. Let her experience help you become spiritually alive in Christ."
—*Tom Donnan, author of five Christian books*

"There are many books being written and published today. So many of them are simply the result of an author with a golden pen and a talent for writing. While Kim Patterson has exhibited literary talent, this book isn't birthed out of just talent or the creative mind of the writer. It is evident that Kim has experienced the touch of the One who's name is the Word of God. She has not only had a powerful ongoing experience in Christ, but she has been gifted by God to be able to express that in a literary way. She makes it clear to the reader how they can come to the same place in God that will give them their own story. Do yourself a favor and read this book and then pass it on to a friend, and they will thank you for it."
—*Dale Everett, Dale Everett Ministries*

"Intimacy with the Father is essential to knowing and understanding who you are in Him. As you journey through this book, Ms. Patterson shares insight into a deeper relationship with God. If you desire the presence of God in your life, at a level that you've never experienced before, this book is for you. As you read page after page of this book, allow the Holy Spirit to minister and lead you to a deeper, more intimate relationship with God."
—*Peggy Cowan, Jeremiah 1:10 Ministries, author of* Living in the Promise

To the Thirsty

JOURNEY INTO THE DEPTHS OF GOD

Kim Patterson

RIVER BIRCH PRESS

Daphne, Alabama

ISBN 978-1-951561-55-0 (Print)
ISBN 978-1-951561-56-7 (Ebook)
For Worldwide Distribution
Printed in the U.S.A.

River Birch Press
P.O. Box 868, Daphne, AL 36526

Dedication

This book is dedicated to my friend Katie Purdy. When I'm in her presence, the spirit inside me leaps, for she is Mary to my Elizabeth. God spoke to her these three words: temple, worship, and wall. It has been an honor to work with her as God taught us the meaning of these words. He brings some people into our lives because they can ignite the fire God has put in us. God has put a burning in my heart for this revelation and message. What I have freely received, I freely give.

This book is the product of the revelation given to me by the Holy Spirit while I was in His presence and by the wisdom I've gained through my personal journey. He has given me the grace to compile it in a way to communicate it concisely, and he has anointed me to write it down so He can pour out His message on anyone who feels led to read it. May it bless you, and may the Holy Spirit transform you as you enter His presence and receive your own revelation.

On the last day, the climax of the festival,
Jesus stood and shouted to the crowds,
"Anyone who is thirsty may come to me!
Anyone who believes in me may come and drink!
For the Scriptures declare,
'Rivers of living water
will flow from his heart.'"
(John 7:37 NLT)

Table of Contents

Introduction

Standing there in the church that day, I had no idea my life was about to change forever. I had attended that church before. In fact, I had attended many churches. But that day, I stood in line to receive a generational blessing, thinking, *Boy, I could sure use that.*

I grew up in a dysfunctional, divorced household. Alcoholism, abuse, pornography, mental illness, and animosity between family members filled my generational bloodline. So that night, I desperately sought a touch from God for my family. Everyone else in church must have needed it just as badly as I did, judging from the length of the prayer line. While I waited, I reflected on my husband and three children and how this generational curse had affected us. I thought about the wife and mother I used to be and how God had transformed me from the controlling, manipulative, perfectionist woman I had been to a woman with a new heart. Ten years of Bible study, devotions, and prayer hadn't been easy, but it had been worth it.

Before my transformation, I had fooled myself into thinking I had a handle on life and that, despite my childhood, I was a good person. However, I wasn't the good mother I thought I was. When I started to read the Bible, I discovered all kinds of things that didn't line up with my thoughts or actions. This troubled me because I couldn't stand not being perfect. God had held a mirror before me, and I didn't like my reflection.

So I chose to adopt God's perspective. That was not easy, and He brought me to some hard crossroads. I had to take my kids out of their private Christian school because I had made it an idol and kept them there out of fear, not faith. I had to move out of a house I loved so God could bring me into my own promised land. I had to trust Him with things I would normally want to control. I had to end a decade of overeating and self-indulgence. (I did not want to do that, by the way.) But every time God made me choose, I picked His way over my own, and He proved faithful. I don't know anyone like Him. That's why I knew He would give me the generational blessing. It just had to work!

I was standing in the line with my sister-in-law and brother-in-law. We chatted a little, even though we were supposed to wait with reverence. I tried, but did I mention the line was long? I couldn't believe I was standing next to her in the first place. You see, I pretty much despised her for the first fifteen years of our relationship because I was jealous of her. She had everything in life that I wanted, and I had to wait and watch (much like this line) as she lived the life I was supposed to have. I referred to her as my nemesis or "my person" (and not in a good way) to the ladies in my Bible study. Yep, even as a Christian, I was not a "good person." I thought she was my exact opposite. I couldn't understand her way of thinking, nor did I want to. I never gave her the benefit of the doubt. She seemed to go out of her way to hurt me and make me mad. The generational curse of animosity toward family members lived on in me.

One day the Lord gently pointed out that I had drawn the first blood in this battle, and I should apologize. No one else could have said that to me. Only God can speak to us in a way that brings conviction to our hearts and leads us to repentance.

It took me a few months, but one day I apologized and

asked for her forgiveness. Our relationship grew after that, and I found out that we think exactly the same way about God. He is our common denominator and the root of the strong friendship we have today. I cannot imagine life without her. Truly, what the enemy means for evil, God uses for good.

I ended up in this long line with her because she thought I should give this church another try. When I first married my husband, we came to this church because his family went there. To tell you the truth, I never felt as if I belonged. I grew up in the Presbyterian church, then I was Methodist for a short time. But this church was Pentecostal, and they were always talking about the Rapture. Of course, I didn't know anything about that.

All I wanted from a church was a place of community. I wanted to meet other people my age and develop new relationships. I already knew the basics and wasn't interested in a spiritual challenge.

So we landed at a seeker-friendly church, where I instantly felt at home. I made new friends, joined a Bible study, and began to grow in my faith. When I read the Bible, I found satisfaction in God for the first time. I began to desire Him more and more until I adjusted my perspective to His. Soon I started leading Bible studies and teaching classes at the church on Sundays. Life had become fulfilling.

Then He said these two words to me that turned my world upside down: "There's more."

What possible "more" could there be? I couldn't get His words out of my head, let alone my spirit. Soon I left the church I loved to search out this "more." I didn't have a clue where to start, so I visited a variety of churches, thinking I would eventually find it. All the churches seemed the same, however, and none of them had anything more to offer.

When I realized I wouldn't find "more" in a building, I gathered some friends and started a Bible study in my home. Our goal was to search out the Holy Spirit and find the "more." Whenever the Lord put something on my heart, He encouraged me to do it in community. If I struggled with an issue, surely others did as well. I knew I was onto something with this Holy Spirit thing, and my hunger for God grew.

The first time I encountered the Holy Spirit, He helped me lose forty-five pounds. I never could have done that on my own, so I knew it was the work of the Holy Spirit. This had to be part of the "more." My sister-in-law said I should come back to her church and listen to their new pastor. Once I heard him, something in my spirit came alive as my spirit recognized the language of "more." The Spirit spoke truth that resonated with my spirit. And it wasn't just the preaching. The worship spoke to me as well. I had found my "more," or so I had thought.

I finally reached the end of this long line. I was about to receive a generational blessing from world-wide evangelist and healer Dale Everett. As I came to the front, I heard him praying over others, sometimes in tongues, sometimes not. I also noticed he had a huge bowl of oil. He dipped his whole hand into that bowl and smeared oil on people's foreheads. I was thinking I was glad I wasn't going anywhere after this because my hair was going to be frightful.

I began to pray because my family needed this generational blessing. As I stood before him, I had no idea this was the last moment of my old life. From then on, everything changed, marked by something "more."

With his hand full of oil, he smeared my forehead and said, "Be filled with the Holy Ghost!"

I took two steps. Waves of tears and uncontrollable weeping overwhelmed me as I became aware of great love. It felt like warmth all over my body, enveloping me. I didn't know what to do with this love. I felt completely vulnerable, as if a light had turned on and exposed all my hurt, pain, remorse, and shame. I could not hold back the flood washing over me and driving out all that hurt.

For an hour, the Holy Spirit ministered to me after He made His explosive entrance. I received the "more" that very night, a "more" that cannot be contained in a building but went with me wherever I went, for it dwells in a temple without walls. The "more" I'd searched for was the "more" that changed my life and is changing my family. Sometimes God makes us wait in a long line to see if we will endure it. Then He can smear us with the "more" of His Spirit.

Here is my prayer for you:

I pray He will fill you and touch you and minister to you as only He can do, knowing you personally and intimately. I pray that as you read this book, the fire of God will fall on you, awakening in you a hunger and thirst for His presence until you sense it all around you. I pray that, out of a great intimacy with the Father, you will come to know Him more, and you will discover who you truly are and His great purpose for you.

I pray that as you sit with Him, He will take you deeper and higher into His love until He births in you a great passion for Him. This passion cannot be quenched. Instead, it propels you into passionate pursuit of God Himself. I pray protection over you as you embark on this journey and dwell in God's presence. I dispatch angels to surround you and guard you against all evil. May the Lord keep you under the protection of His wing. May He uphold you with His mighty right hand and keep you secure and safe, hidden from the enemy in the secret place.

❧ Foundation ❧

TEMPLE – WORSHIP – WALL

≈ *One* ≈

THE CROSS OF VICTORY

It occurred to me a few years ago that, although I was a Christian, I didn't experience the victory Christ bought for me on the cross. How many of you would say you walk in complete victory in your life, your relationships, your body, and your finances? Did you know that victory is ours? It's not just a neat Christian saying. If Jesus died on the cross and shed His blood so we could be free and live in victory, why don't we?

Jesus said, "If anyone come after me, he must deny himself and take up his cross and follow me" (Matthew 16:24). I want to propose that the cross we've been picking up is the "old rugged cross," the one Jesus was crucified on and which holds all our sins and curses. The cross He means for us to pick up is the cross of victory. He died on the old rugged cross so we wouldn't have to. He never meant us to pick up that cross, but we do—every day. No, He gave us the cross of victory, by which He conquered the enemy. In it we find power, healing, abundance—all we need to live in victory and follow in His footsteps.

This is what He meant when He said, "Follow me; deny

yourself" (Matthew 16:24). Deny who the enemy says you are. Stop taking ownership of those labels. You are a new creation in Christ (2 Corinthians 5:17). "For whoever wants to save his life will lose it, but whoever loses his life for me will find it" (Matthew 16:25). Would you give up who the enemy says you are? Will you die to that person, instead becoming who God says you are, rising out of the grave and living in victory? "What good will it be for a man if he gains the whole world, yet forfeits his soul? What can a man exchange for his soul?" (Matthew 16:26). I don't know about you, but I'm exchanging the old rugged cross for the cross of victory.

The Israelites were held in captivity in Babylon for seventy years. How old are you? How many more years do you want to live in captivity? That's where we are if we're not walking in complete victory. Does our enemy hold you in bondage? This could be in your health, your finances, your marriage, your addictions, or numerous other places. The whole time, Satan says, "You're fine right where you are. You're never going to have better than this. You don't deserve anything better. You're blessed, so don't worry about it!"

Oh, did I strike a nerve with that last one? Guess what, when the enemy talks to you, he speaks your language, using words you understand.

How do we come out of bondage? Jesus won the victory on the cross, but we have to enforce it. From creation, God chose to partner with man. He doesn't force His will upon us. We have to choose to cooperate with Him. All authority in heaven and on earth has been given to us, but He gave us the keys to the kingdom of heaven (Matthew 16:18-19).

He does not transform us into His image so we can be the best people we can be. No, we need to walk in victory so we can help others come out of captivity. Before Jesus' ascension, He commissioned us to continue His ministry (Mark 16:15-18, John 14:12-14). You can find His ministry outlined in Isaiah 61. Jesus was anointed to preach the good news, bind up the brokenhearted, proclaim freedom for the captives, and release the prisoners from darkness while proclaiming the year of the Lord's favor. This is the year of the Lord's favor for your life.

You might think you already do all the right things. You go to church, and you pray and read your Bible. You may even read a devotional, volunteer at church, or belong to a Bible study group, but feel like you're not making progress. The enemy has you busy with religious activities, but the Lord has a divine order. When you follow His divine order, you begin to walk in step with Him and enter into the rhythm of heaven.

When the Jews returned from Babylon to Jerusalem, they needed to rebuild their temple, reinstate worship, and repair the wall that established the city and protected them from their enemies. That's exactly what we need to do but within the layers of divine order that will bring us deeper into the well of God's presence. I hope you will have your own personal encounter with the Holy Spirit.

Journey into the well and discover your Temple-Worship-Wall!

≈ *Two* ≈

THE WELL OF HIS PRESENCE

After Jesus's crucifixion, God the Father tore the temple veil so we could enter the Holy of Holies (Matthew 27:51). Now we can come into God's presence. In the Old Testament, only the high priest could enter the Holy of Holies, and then only one time per year as he made atonement for the whole nation of Israel. When Jesus died on the cross, the earth shook and the temple veil tore from top to bottom. This symbolized that nothing separated us from God anymore because Jesus made the atonement once and for all. Therefore, we can boldly enter heaven's most holy place because of the blood of Jesus (Hebrews 10:19 NLT). Now everyone can come into God's presence.

Entering God's presence, however, is not symbolic or theoretical. I used to believe coming into God's presence was symbolic. When I prayed, in theory, I pictured myself standing in front of Him. I also thought of it as a judicial position, as I now had the legal right to come into His presence, because Jesus made the way. While that is true, it doesn't come close to the full meaning. God's presence is an actual position. You can come into His presence and know He is with you. You can feel Him and sense Him. When you are in His presence, He gives you things you cannot get anywhere else. He gives you everything you need. It's sad that many Christians miss this type of fellowship with God because they don't understand that His presence is real.

By his death, Jesus opened a new and life giving way through the curtain. Into the Most Holy Place. And since we have a great High Priest who rules over God's house, let us go right into the presence of God with sincere hearts fully trusting him (Hebrews 10:20-22 NLT).

About two years ago, I went on a mission to discover what it meant to be in God's presence. I heard people say, "Oh, the presence of God is here," or "I could feel the presence of God today." Or my favorite: "I was hit with the presence of God." I didn't have a clue what they were talking about, but I was pretty sure they weren't making it up. And I certainly wanted this "presence."

Guess what? God wants you in His presence too. He desires intimate fellowship with you in His presence. He longs for fellowship with everyone. He loves us and desires to be with us. Soon I began to read *Practicing His Presence* by Brother Lawrence and Frank Laibach and *The Pursuit of God: A 31-Day Experience* by A.W. Tozer. I committed to do the things the books said to do, all with anticipation of encountering His presence. And boy, did I ever! My life is forever changed by encountering and experiencing the living God.

When His presence shows up, you will know it. Second Chronicles chapter five tells us what happened when the Ark of the Covenant was brought back to the temple. The ark is where the God of Israel lived. King Solomon built the temple so God would have a permanent residence with His people. There was great fanfare when they brought the ark to the temple. It was a big deal and a huge celebration with musicians, singers, and priests. Here's what happened when they set the ark in the Holy of Holies:

Then the temple of the Lord was filled with a cloud, and the priests could not perform their services because of the cloud, and the glory of the Lord filled the temple of God (2 Chronicles 5:13-14).

This was not a subtle thing. It did not go unnoticed that God's presence and glory had just shown up. The temple was filled—boom! God just entered the building. He entered in such a way that no one could continue what they'd been doing just a second before.

That's not to say this will happen every time we get into God's presence. But we'll notice He is there. We are the New Testament temple. First Corinthians 6:19 says, "Do you not know that your body is a temple of the Holy Spirit who is in you, whom you have received from God?" So if God shows up in your temple, you'll notice. You get into God's presence when you decide to bring God into your temple, just as Solomon brought the ark into the temple and put it in its proper place (the heart of the temple). When you decide to seat God on the throne of your heart, you put Him in His proper place in your temple, giving Him the opportunity to fill you with His presence and glory.

We sometimes feel God's presence physically. You may feel a lump in your throat, a fullness in your head, or a heaviness in your chest. You may also feel tingling on your skin in different areas of your body or see colors swirling in your mind's eye. These are just a few examples. You may feel something completely different. Just as we all look different, we will experience the Holy Spirit differently. Sometimes the Holy Spirit may manifest Himself through tears, laughter, or a shaking in a particular part of your body, such as hands or legs. This is not a checklist to help you determine whether you are in God's presence. They are merely possibilities for you to anticipate.

Begin to train your senses to feel the Holy Spirit. Hebrews 5:14 (BSB) says, "Solid food is for the mature, who by constant use have trained their senses." Learn how the Holy Spirit feels on your body or in your spirit when you get into His presence. This is called the tangible presence of God, and it must be cultivated in order to sense it.

When Pastor Dale Everett anointed me with oil and told me, "Be filled with the Holy Ghost," I knew I was immediately filled, because my tears flowed uncontrollably. I was not sad, but I could not stop the tears. This went on for an hour. I didn't understand what was happening, but I knew it was the Holy Spirit. I was afraid that, when I left that church, He would leave me. I was not about to let that happen. Now I realize He was ministering to me.

When you get into His presence, God will give you exactly what you need. He may bring revelation, fulfillment, joy, peace, or clarity. In His presence you will find grace, honor, mercy, faithfulness, and gladness. His presence is a place of shelter, protection, and safety. He will reveal and remove the things that don't belong to Him. When you get into His presence, He reveals, and when you stay in His presence, He ministers. Don't rush out of the presence. Make sure you stay in the stillness until you've received what He wants to give you.

When we're in His presence, He tells us who we are and establishes our identity. Look what Colossians 3:3-4 of the Passion Translation says:

Your crucifixion with Christ has severed the tie to this life, and now your true life is hidden away in God in Christ. And as Christ himself is seen for who he really is, who you really are will also be revealed, for you are now one with him in his glory!

Your true identity is hidden away in God, and He will reveal it to you when you're "one with him in his glory." That place is His presence, and He invites us to remain there. We should become so mature and trained that His presence (the Holy Spirit) remains on us as we go about our day. This training begins with one question: how much do we want it?

The desire to pursue God originates with Him because He is the initiator of everything. I did not pursue Him first, but He put it in my heart to seek His presence. God makes a move toward us, and the next move is ours. Our response is up to us and makes all the difference in the world.

As the deer pants for streams of water, so my soul pants for you, my God. My soul thirsts for God, for the living God. When can I go and meet with God? (Psalm 42:1-2)

We must search for Him with this type of hunger and thirst. The Bible promises that when we search for Him with all our hearts, we will find Him. But He wants our whole heart. I think the Christian religion has put too much emphasis on merely saying a neat little prayer, and that makes the whole process of conversion mechanical and spiritless.

In his book The Pursuit of God, A.W. Tozer said, "Christ may be 'received' without creating any special love for Him in the soul of the receiver. The man is 'saved,' but he is not hungry nor thirsty after God. In fact, he is specifically taught to be satisfied. And is encouraged to be content with little." God has much more for us than this. But only the person who hungers and thirsts for the Living God will find it. As John 7:37 (BSB) says, "Anyone who is thirsty, let him come and drink." Streams of living water will flow from the person who hungers and thirsts for God. The living water is the Holy Spirit. To understand this fully, we need to look at the first passage in which He mentioned this living water: the woman at the well in John chapter four.

Jesus was tired from His journey and sat down next to Jacob's Well. A Samaritan woman came to the well, and Jesus asked her for a drink. Because she is a Samaritan, she said, "How can you ask me for a drink?"

That simply wasn't done in that day. She knew He was a Jew, and she knew Jews didn't associate with Samaritans. But Jesus answered, "If you knew the gift of God and who it is that asks you for a drink, you would have asked him and he would have given you living water" (John 4:10).

Of course, Jesus was no longer talking about regular water. He was talking about the spiritual refreshment only the Holy Spirit can provide—the water that quenches our thirsty souls.

She answers, "You have nothing to draw with and the well is deep" (John 4:11). I love her response, such a reflection of the state of her soul. Haven't we all felt that way? But Jesus knew He had something to draw the water. He had her! This was His first invitation to go deep into the presence of God. With it He gave us a prophetic picture of the way we are all to come to the well of His presence.

You see, Jesus is the well. He didn't tell the woman He would be the drink. No, the Holy Spirit is the living water, but Jesus has it and can give it. When we come to the well, we encounter Jesus, and when we dip into the well, He gives us the Holy Spirit. While in the well (His presence), the Spirit gives us something to carry. Picture it! The woman is the vessel to draw from the well. We are the vessels!

What He gives us to carry is personal to us, but He wants us to pour it out on others. We must first carry it for ourselves, letting it minister to us. Once we've received it for ourselves, we can then share it. He may put someone in our path who will need what we've received. Anything we are given must be given away. "Freely you have received; freely give," (Matthew 10:8). If He gives us something to carry, He gives us the grace to walk it out and the anointing to pour it out. Look at John 4:29. The woman went into the town and said, "Come, see the man who told me everything I ever did. Could this be the Christ?"

She did not have the reputation or the credibility to deliver that message. No one would have believed her if God had not given grace. And look what happened in verse 39: "Many of the Samaritans from that town believed in him because of the woman's testimony." They didn't believe because she had credibility. In fact, it was the complete opposite. They believed because she had an anointing to pour out her message. When we come to the well of His presence, we encounter Jesus, and the Holy Spirit gives us something to carry. The deeper we go into His presence, the more He gives us until we reach the rivers of living water. But going deeper is a process, and we can't get to the deepest part without first going through the shallows. There is a divine order to diving deep. We can find treasures in every layer.

Take your time in each layer. Do not try to rush out quickly. Study, worship, and pray that layer. Linger and hunt for every treasure God has for you. "It's the glory of God to conceal a thing; but the honor of the kings is to search out a matter" (Proverbs 25:2 KJV). He has hidden His secrets in order that you would "seek and find." What a joy to go on a great treasure hunt with God. You will feel a release and a pressing and great satisfaction when it's time to go deeper. At the same time, you'll sense dissatisfaction that only a deeper drink can quench. Jesus' invitation is TO THE THIRSTY. . . Come and drink!

⌇ *Three* ⌇

DIVINE ORDER

When the Jewish people returned to Jerusalem after their captivity in Babylon, they discovered that God's temple needed to be rebuilt (Ezra 6:3-5, Zechariah 6:12-13,15). Worship needed to be reinstated (Ezra 4:10-11), and the wall surrounding the city needed to be repaired (Nehemiah 2:17). We must do the same things as we leave behind our own captivity.

God allowed the Babylonians to take Israel into captivity because recent generations had stopped relying on God. They no longer followed the Lord, turning instead to idol worship. They put other gods before the One True God (Exodus 20). They had forgotten who God was and what He had done for them as a nation. So He allowed a conquering army to take them from their Promised Land and drag them into captivity, where they became slaves and servants to the Babylon empire.

Satan is our Babylon. When we stop relying on God and following Him, and when other things (like money, pride, and self) replace God on the throne of our hearts, we give the enemy permission to make us slaves to those things and servants to him. The enemy has chained us in many areas of our lives. The only way out is to recognize our need for God and to pray for Him to show us the way home.

After Israel had lived in captivity for seventy years, God brought them out of Babylon and led them home to Jerusalem. You can read about this return in the books of Ezra, Nehemiah, and Zechariah. But after seventy years, their homes lay in shambles, which is exactly how we feel after the enemy has done his damage. The temple, which was God's home among His people, needed to be rebuilt so God's presence could return.

Until I had children, I didn't see how this damage affected all areas of my life. I can trace my captivity all the way back to my childhood and because of the havoc the enemy was wreaking in my parents' lives. When I became a parent, I duplicated my mom's parenting style because she was my example. But she was a single parent, and I was married. I had to re-evaluate what it meant to be a mother, in order to become a godly mother. The enemy would have loved for me to stay in the performance trap, parenting out of control and punishment instead of giving grace and godly discipline.

We need to build up our temple and make it fit to house the Holy Spirit. Our "junk" not only holds us captive, but it also makes us unfit to house His presence. Certain activities can help us to become more fit. Just as an unhealthy body can benefit from exercise, we need the exercises of worship, reading the Bible, and prayer in order to become spiritually fit.

The returning captives had forgotten how to worship God. They had forgotten what was in His Word. Most of them didn't remember how to pray, because they had stopped doing it long ago. But God had positioned leaders and prophets who prayed for them, began to teach them the Word, and eventually brought worship back into their daily lives.

I'll bet you have someone like that in your life, who has been praying for you all this time. I'm sure they are a good source of support and information. I was fortunate to have two godly, praying women who lifted me up and encouraged me in the Word.

As we rebuild, we need to worship, read, and pray. This does not happen overnight. You will encounter great opposition. Hecklers, naysayers, and bullies wanted to stop the Israelites from experiencing God's presence, and you'll face them too. The enemy will come against you from every side, so you'll need to learn to build and protect yourself at the same time. That's why the Jews held a trowel in one hand and a sword in the other as they repaired the wall around the city.

The Bible is both trowel and sword. As you read God's Word, it builds you up. It builds your faith, your knowledge, and your identity while it protects you from the enemy. The Word is also called the Sword of the Spirit because, as you speak God's Word and release His promises over your life, the enemy takes a blow. It cuts him to the core, just as it cuts you to the core as you read it.

For the word of God is quick, and powerful, and sharper than any two-edged sword, piercing even to the dividing asunder of soul and spirit, and of the joints and marrow, and is discerner of the thoughts and intents of the heart. (Hebrews 4:12 KJV)

Layers of Divine Order

According to Ezra 6:4, the temple has four layers: three of stone and one of timber. As I began researching this book, before I had come across this verse, my friend Katie and I wondered why God called us to study. The Lord then showed me the word "order," and I saw it repeated four times. Rather than running horizontally, as words usually do, God showed them to me vertically, one on top of the other. I soon learned that we are built in layers as the temple was, but we are also transformed in layers.

As we go deeper into His presence, we pass through four layers of water. These layers are God's divine order. He is a God of order, not chaos. But His order may look different than our order. For instance, we might think we need to get our act together before we come to Him. However, He calls us to come just as we are, for while we were still sinners, Jesus died for us (Romans 5:8).

That isn't how things usually work in the world. In fact, if something doesn't sound logical, it is probably God. Put aside what you have learned and be open to His divine order. His order says the spiritual comes first. Most of us want to do that last. This is man's order: First, I will get a higher education, then I will work on my health because I neglected it for too many years. Last, I will read the Bible because the Lord could take me at any minute, and I want to be ready.

But when you first have spiritual order, your mind is renewed, and you have mental order because you have the mind of Christ. Once you have spiritual and mental order, you have physical order because your body begins to line up as you take authority over your health. And last, divine order begins to shape your circumstances. If your circumstances are out of control and you are plagued with problems, perhaps you have things out of order. For example, you cannot operate in principles from Layer Three if you haven't attained what you needed in Layer Two. You can study these principles all you want. You can even apply what you've learned, but if you try to do it out of order, you may not see the fruit of your efforts. You may feel the frustration of having no results or feeling inadequate. You are not inadequate. You just aren't there yet in your journey. I hope this brings freedom to someone today.

The layers of His divine order help us to go deeper into God's presence as we apply temple, worship, and wall to our layers. Each layer needs to be developed in our journey, but only in the divine order God uses. That way, we can be effective on our journey.

We cannot dig a well without first passing through all the layers of soil. We start at the top and go down deeper and deeper. In Ezekiel 47:1-6, Ezekiel describes water that flows from all sides of the temple. It starts out ankle deep, then it becomes knee deep, then waist deep, until finally it's a river. What starts as a trickle ends with a flowing river you must swim in.

Don't despise small beginnings or shallow starts. God values them highly. But He doesn't want you to stay there. He wants you to move out into the deep. That is what it's like in the well. We move from the shallow surface into the depths of God's presence. God must work through and in us what He wants to accomplish in each layer before we can move on to the next layer. When we work in His divine order, we will experience more satisfaction, freedom, and power in our journey with Him.

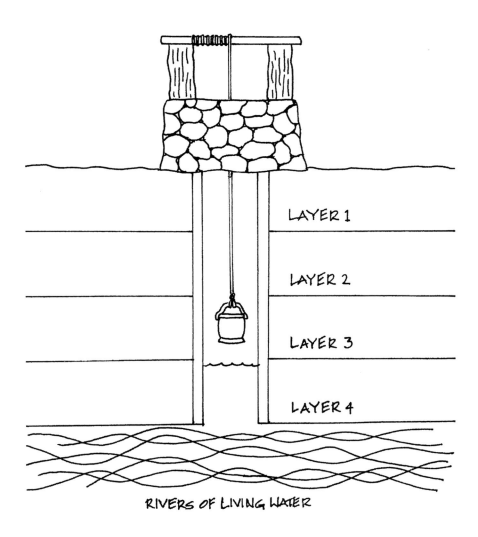

RIVERS OF LIVING WATER

Understanding Temple, Worship, Wall

Let's take a closer look at the concept of Temple, Worship, Wall and discover what they represent so we can understand how they affect each layer. Their representation is the same in each layer, but the way we apply them is different.

The Temple is how we relate to and partner with the Holy Spirit. Our bodies are the temple for the Holy Spirit (1 Corinthians 6:19). Jesus says in Revelation 3:20, "Here I am! I stand at the door and knock. If anyone hears my voice and opens the door, I will come in and eat with him, and he with me." This is Jesus inviting us to respond to His voice and presence and to partner with Him in relationship. As our relationship deepens, it affects our interactions with the Holy Spirit. As we learn to yield to Him more and more, He uses us in different ways.

Now let's examine Worship. In the layers, worship represents both prayer and worship. How we pray and worship is different in each layer and changes as our relationship deepens. In the Old Testament, the priests filled censers with coals and incense. Then they lit them with sacrificial fire, and the smoke rose as a pleasing fragrance to the Lord. This represented the Israelites' prayers (Leviticus 16:12-13). Psalm 141:2 says, "May my prayer be set before you like incense; may the lifting up of my hands be like the evening sacrifice." God desires both the lifting of our prayers and worship. You will notice this reference again in Revelation:

And when he had taken it, the four living creatures and the twenty-four elders fell down before the Lamb. Each one had a harp and they were holding golden bowls full of

19

incense, which are the prayers of the saints (Revelation 5:8).

In this verse, the creatures held harps (representing worship) and bowls of incense (representing prayers). This shows us that worship and prayer go hand in hand. We should not do one without the other. In the layers, we will use the censer as a metaphor for our prayers and see how it changes in each layer as we get closer to Him.

The Wall protects and establishes us. This also changes in each of the layers. As we become more established, how we're protected is different. The time has come for us to rebuild our ancient ruins and restore the places long devastated (Isaiah 61:4). Isaiah also says this about us:

Your people will rebuild the ancient ruins and will raise up the age-old foundations; you will be called Repairer of Broken Walls, Restorer of Streets with Dwellings (Isaiah 58:12).

We all have built walls that we think protect us. But we build them on faulty foundations established by the world. Those walls need to come down, and new walls need to go up on the foundation that is the Rock (Matthew 7:24-27 ESV). In the layers, we will explore this process. As we repair and rebuild our own walls, we begin to help others, and then God sends His divine protection.

Through the layers of His divine order, "we all, who with unveiled faces contemplate the Lord's glory, are being transformed into his image with ever-increasing glory, which comes from the Lord, who is the Spirit" (2 Corinthians

3:18). We are moving within the layers from faith to faith (little faith to great faith), from strength to strength (our strength to His strength), and from glory to glory. We are the glory of His creation revealed. As we grow, we begin to display more of His glory. The message in 2 Corinthians 3:18 reflects an endless possibility for growth and transformation, for depth and elevation, and for empowerment and glorification. It is the "more" of God. "No eye has seen, no ear has heard, and no mind has imagined what God has prepared for those who love him" (1 Corinthians 2:9 NLT).

Again, it comes down to this question: How much do you want it?

Layer One

POSITIONING OUR HEARTS AND DYING TO SELF

✑ Four ✑

TEMPLE: GOD IS ON THE THRONE OF MY LIFE

In the year King Uzziah died, I saw the Lord seated on the throne, high and exalted (Isaiah 6:1 BSB).

Do you have someone you look up to or idolize? It could be a parent, mentor, or leader. Isaiah looked up to King Uzziah. Uzziah was one of Judah's good kings. He sought God and did what was pleasing in the Lord's sight. He cared about building and farming, as well as forming and maintaining a strong army. His fame spread far, for the Lord gave him marvelous help and made him very powerful (2 Chronicles 26:15 NLT).

When someone like this dies, we can feel lost. It is only when our idols die (figuratively) that we can see God in His rightful place. We may think we don't need God because we already have someone to look up to. We don't follow Him wholeheartedly because we're already following someone or something else. Idols are anything or anyone we put in the place of God—anything or anyone we trust instead of God. Isaiah saw the Lord seated on the throne only after his idol died. We need to place God on the throne of our hearts if we want to see Him or encounter Him. We must make Him our king.

This is a hard concept for Americans, since we don't have royalty. We don't understand the role of a king, and we don't see a need for one. So let's take a look at the role of a king. A king rules over and protects a land or nation. He is the spiritual focus and a man of war. He is the national stronghold. The ruler is a source of identification and role model for the society. He delivers justice and cannot allow himself to compromise. His law is absolute. The king should have authority, dignity, humility, wisdom, and moral integrity.

Considering this, it's not hard to see God as the King of kings. But most of us don't want a king, because we already have one. Something already sits on the throne of our hearts, and in order to see God on the throne, we must dethrone our idol.

Dear children, keep away from anything that might take God's place in your hearts (1 John 5:21 NLT).

For a lot of us, this idol can be money, control, our career, spouse, or even our children. But the most common idol that sits on the throne of hearts is ourselves, and we don't even realize it.

When I was in my thirties, life was good. I had gotten most of the things I wanted out of life at that time: a wonderful husband, a nice house, three great kids—and I was in control of it all. I was sitting pretty on my throne in the kingdom I had created with my goals and hard work. Why did I need the Lord over my life? I was doing pretty well already.

But it was impossible to live up to being lord of my own life, and I wasn't doing a good job. It became harder and harder for me to "reign over my kingdom," so I started to look to other things for security, protection, and identity. I put more "idols" on the throne and looked to them to save me. For me, it was money, a Christian school for my kids, and the appearance of myself and my home. I started to feel less and less satisfied and more and more frustrated.

God is the rightful King. Anything else is an idol and we need to sacrifice it. We need to lay it down because it has no power (Jeremiah 10:15). It is useless (1 Samuel 12:21) and keeps us from turning to God when things go wrong.

Recently, I allowed an idol to slip onto the throne of my heart. When I realized what I'd done, I was shocked and saddened to think I wasn't putting God first. I thought I had laid down my idols, but it's easy for them to creep back into our hearts. Ridding our hearts of idols isn't a one-time thing. We must constantly evaluate our hearts and get rid of the idols.

I had just lost a lot of weight. I knew the Holy Spirit wanted me to do that, and He helped me. I couldn't have done it without His power. I had been maintaining that weight loss for about a year when I began to admire my new looks. When I went shopping, everything looked good on me. I was not used to that. I started to spend too much money on my wardrobe so I could dress up this new body, focusing on myself too much. God gently pointed out that I had made an idol of my body. I was worshipping something He had given me instead of worshipping Him.

I had to dethrone that idol. I surrendered my body once again and put on ten pounds. I had to trust God to keep me healthy, because I didn't want to fall back into my old bad habits. I took my focus off my body and put it where it should've been all along: on God.

This is why the Bible says we should die to self, which means we surrender ourselves to God. We must lay down our plans, lay down our way of thinking and acting, and allow God to guide our steps and renew our thinking. This is where we learn to follow instead of lead and to walk in trust and obedience. God will protect us because He is just. He reigns with power (Jeremiah 10:6-7) and rules with wisdom and integrity (Jeremiah 10:12-13). He is the only King who can tell us who we are (Acts 17:28). Sacrifice your idols and see the Lord seated on the throne, high and exalted.

Once you see Him, don't take your eyes off Him. It's easy to see Him and then slip into old habits, turning to your old place of comfort. When the Israelites left Egypt, they soon began to grumble, wanting to return to Egypt. The desert was harsh, and they were uncomfortable. They wanted to return to what they knew, even though it meant returning to slavery. As we leave captivity, we will be tempted to return because the enemy tries hard to convince us that's where we belong. When things get tough, it will feel natural to turn to our old idols.

We need to take our eyes off our circumstances and see God instead. The Israelites saw only what they lacked. They didn't see God giving them guidance and protection. He appeared to them as a pillar of clouds by day so they would know where to go. He appeared as a pillar of fire by night for guidance and protection. He provided water from a rock and manna to eat. They collected this manna every day as a reminder to keep their eyes on God.

We need to learn that lesson as well. If we want to see

God's provision, we must seek Him every day in His word and in prayer for direction and sustenance. Jesus said:

Seek first his kingdom and his righteousness, and all these things will be given to you as well (Matthew 6:33).

What are "all these things"? Look back at verse 25: "Do not worry about your life, what you will eat or drink; or about your body, what you will wear." He's talking about the everyday cares of life. When you seek God first and make Him your priority, He provides for your everyday needs. Do not look at what you think you lack. Look instead to your King, who you have put on your throne and who will meet all your needs according to the riches in Christ Jesus (Philippians 4:19).

When you focus on Him and His goodness, you'll respond with thankfulness. This attitude of sacrifice and thankfulness positions our hearts to come to Him in the first layer of prayer and begins the process of dying to self.

❧ *Five* ❧

WORSHIP: SURRENDER MYSELF AND LAY MY BURDENS AT THE CROSS

Offer your bodies as living sacrifices, holy and pleasing to God—this is your spiritual act of worship (Romans 12:1).

In Layer One, sacrifice is worship. When the Israelites brought sacrifices to the temple, they were obeying, honoring, and worshipping God. We cannot worship Him properly if we're not willing to sacrifice ourselves to Him. God isn't asking us to do anything that He hasn't already done for us. Remember, everything originates with God. "We love because God first loved us" (1 John 4:19), and we can sacrifice because God first sacrificed. We only need to look at the cross to see this sacrifice, but it is meant as a gift to us. When we can see sacrifice as a gift, it helps to change the lens through which we view sacrifice. In order to see this, let's go back to Jesus' birth where we were first given Him as a gift— God's gift to the world. The secret to this gift was in the wrapping.

This will be a sign to you: You will find a baby wrapped in cloths and lying in a manger" (Luke 2:12).

The NLT says He was wrapped snugly in strips of cloths or swaddled. When traveling on long journeys, Jewish people would carry strips of cloth with them. Mary was not carrying them because she needed something to wrap the baby in when He was born. She was carrying them because traveling was dangerous, and they could have come across a dead body or possibly either one of them could have died on the journey. It was against Jewish law for a Jew to touch a dead body for they would become unclean (Numbers 19:11). To not risk contamination, they would use the cloths to wrap the body. When Jesus was born, He was wrapped in these cloths— burial cloths. Jesus was born to die for you and me. God's great gift was a sacrifice. What then should our gift to God be? A gift of sacrifice.

The sacrifice You desire is a broken spirit, You will not reject a broken and repentant heart, O God (Psalm 51:17).

Of course, I am referring to a spiritual sacrifice that involves surrendering our bodies and will to His. Surrendering our bodies means giving Him permission to cleanse us, purify our hearts, and transform us until we are holy as He is holy (1 Peter 1:16).

The sin in our lives makes us unfit to house His presence. We must let God convict us of the sin that hinders us. Our sin keeps us bound to the enemy. As God reveals this sin, we need to resist feeling offended or defensive. Instead, we need to see God's perspective and repent (have a new mindset about it and begin to walk in the opposite direction). Then God can purify our hearts. As we submit to God and turn from sin, the enemy will flee from us (James 4:7), and the chains that bind us to sin will begin to fall off.

When we surrender our will, we give Him access to our emotions and mind so He can heal us and transform the way we think. Then we can walk in righteousness. We must surrender every day, align our thoughts and actions with His, and give Him complete control over every aspect of our lives.

This may seem frightening, but Jesus promises that His yoke is easy and His burden is light (Matthew 11:30). We all wear a yoke (something that is placed around our necks to direct us). This yoke might be a responsibility or obligation someone else puts on us, or we can place it on ourselves. Trying to be perfect, I have had to put so many yokes around my own neck. Because of circumstances in my childhood, I believed I must be perfect before people can see value in me. My appearance, along with my house and my children, had to seem perfect to anyone looking on. I had to plan everything down to the last detail, so events and schedules would go off without problems. If anything went wrong, it meant I was not perfect in my planning.

I also had yokes that others put on me. For example, one yoke told me I wasn't doing enough. I should work outside the home and help with my family's financial needs.

These yokes can be demanding and burdensome, but Jesus promises rest to all who come to Him. If we put on His yoke and learn from Him a little each day, we can't help but worship Him by surrendering ourselves to this rest. We can die to self only with God's help as we daily come to Him in full surrender.

One of the things we need to surrender every day is our prayer list as we cast our cares on Him. We cannot hold onto our worries and anxieties. If we do, they become added weight to the yoke around our neck, and they distract us from this rest.

Cast all your anxiety on Him because he cares for you (1 Peter 5:7).

Do not be anxious about anything, but in everything by prayer and supplication with thanksgiving let your requests be made known to God (Philippians 4:6 ESV).

If you don't feel different after you've released your cares to the Lord, then you didn't release them. All you did was vent or complain to God. That's all right. He is compassionate enough to handle all your venting and complaining, but you are robbing yourself of the rest He wants you to have. The sooner you learn to release, the sooner you can move on to Layer Two praying.

The Censer

In the Old Testament, the priests used brass or bronze censers when they prayed. They filled the censer with live coals from the sacrificial altar, then they threw in sweet incense. Then a cloud of smoke arose and filled the air with fragrance (Leviticus 16:12-13). This was a symbolic act of releasing the prayers of the people.

If we use this same symbol of the censer as an analogy of how our prayers rise, we will see that our surrender is like the coals from the altar. When we pray, it is as if we throw our incense (prayers) onto the coals. The fire from our sacrifice enables our prayers to rise as a pleasing aroma to the Lord. As our prayers rise, the smoke dissipates, representing the carrying away of our burden, worry, and anxiety.

As we move through the layers, we will examine our prayers' functions. In Layer One, it is important to see the correlation between surrender and release. There can be no release without surrender. The more we hold onto, the less likely we are to enter into the promise of His rest.

How should our prayers look in this layer? First, invite the Holy Spirit to come. Wait a few seconds to allow your spirit to quiet. When you are still, you can focus on God. Worship Him with your sacrifice. You can pray something like, "Lord, I give You this time and this day. Have Your way. Do what You want to do; say what You want to say. Help me to go where You want me to go today."

Your praise is your sacrifice. Because of your anxiety and worry, you may not feel like thanking Him or praising Him, so say something like, "Lord, I don't feel like praising You today, but I'm going to because I know You're good. I know I can trust You, and I know You are faithful."

You can also offer yourself as a sacrifice. You might say something like this: "Lord, I give You myself. Work in me and make me who You created me to be." Once you've brought your sacrifice to Him, surrender all your cares. Tell Him everything that bothers you and causes you anxiety. Tell Him everything that has your mind and heart tied up in knots. Ask Him for the things you need from Him.

As you do this, picture these cares rising like a balloon. Watch it go higher and higher until you cannot see the balloon or your cares anymore. Expect in faith that He has received them and is carrying them away so you don't have to be concerned anymore. Then thank Him for taking them and for the resolution and answer He will provide. Thank Him for the peace and rest He is giving you. Then sit in silence and stillness, knowing He is God, and He cares for you. Meditate on His love, provision, wisdom, and goodness. Wait to see if He speaks to you or reveals anything to you. He might give you a new thought or a quiet knowing of something new. It might be a new feeling in your gut. Learn to recognize His voice (the various ways God communicates to you). It may take a while at first, but as you learn to hear Him, you'll recognize His voice and be able to follow His leading (John 10:1-5). Anticipate God speaking to you. Wait for a release in your spirit and say, "Amen."

WALL: DEMOLISH MY STRONGHOLDS

Do not conform any longer to the pattern of this world, but be transformed by the renewing of your mind (Romans 12:2).

Life has a way of shaping our identity. Our circumstances and education can slant our perspective, and our relationships sometimes leave us wounded. As we get older, these experiences, along with the world, begin to form our actions, thoughts, and relationships. We develop ways to protect ourselves from getting hurt. We build walls around our heart so certain things and people can't get in. Soon we learn not to be vulnerable or transparent because people use it against us. We put up the same walls in our minds to protect our ideas, dreams, values, and beliefs.

Do you want to know how the enemy starts the process of leading us into captivity? He gets us to do it for him. He is in the world. He gets us to react to him in the world—and we build the walls. We separate ourselves, trying to feel safe. We become prisoners inside our walls. Then he provides attractive alternatives that we think will help us cope with our frustrations and loneliness. We take the bait, and he reels us in.

My parents divorced when I was about ten years old. The abandonment wounded me. Determined not to let my father hurt me again, I built a wall around my heart, refusing to let him get close. I built a wall in my mind, believing all men eventually leave. Therefore, I lived each day waiting for that to happen. I never trusted men, and I never felt safe in relationships. However, I desperately needed security, so I hid inside my walls of protection, believing I could depend on no one but myself.

Can you see the pattern? As a prisoner within my own walls for many years, I had no relationship with my father and an insecure relationship with my husband. I had put all men into a box of my own making. I even put God in that box. I couldn't relate to Him as Father. It was hard for me to trust Him not to leave me too, especially when I needed Him. The answer was not to need men or God.

Do you see how the enemy used that one event to shape me? What has shaped you? Can you apply this same pattern to something in your life? Have you had enough? If so, decide to put God on the throne, and begin the process of letting Him establish you and protect you. We no longer need the walls of lies we've built. It says in Psalm 119:29 of the *New Living Translation*, "Keep me from lying to myself; give me the privilege of knowing your instructions." This has got to be our prayer. We must begin the process of bringing the walls down, but that can be easier said than done. God and His word is the only One who can help us.

Earlier, we discussed the temple veil that tore when Jesus died. But there is another kind of veil—the one that separates our minds from the mind of Christ. The enemy uses this veil to blind us and keep us from the knowledge of God.

The natural man does not accept the things of the Spirit of God; for they are foolishness to him; and he cannot understand them (1 Corinthians 2:14 BSB).

The god of this world has blinded the minds of the unbelievers, to keep them from seeing the light of the gospel of the glory of Christ, who is the image of God (2 Corinthians 4:4 ESV).

As we read God's Word, He changes our perspective until it lines up with His. We get to know Him through His Word, and we get to know how He sees us, which is different from what the world tells us. When we learn the truth and it penetrates our hearts and minds, the truth frees us from the enemy's chains (John 8:32). The veil is lifted and we proclaim, "Once I was blind, but now I see" (John 9:25).

The enemy will fight this process. It will become a real war as you question all the opinions, beliefs, and arguments you once believed. Second Corinthians says this about the war:

We use God's mighty weapons, not worldly weapons, to knock down the strongholds of human reasoning and to destroy false arguments. We destroy every proud obstacle that keeps people from knowing God. We capture their rebellious thoughts and teach them to obey Christ (2 Corinthians 10:4-5 NLT).

The Bible is one of the weapons we use to fight the

enemy in order to take down these strongholds in our minds. A stronghold is a wall or fortress. We can replace this old fortress with God. "The name of the Lord is a strong fortress; the godly run to him and are safe" (Proverbs 18:10 NLT).

Your mind and heart are safe with God. Many of us, however, have gone through some terrible experiences, and they've left us scarred. God wants to heal all our hurts. We cannot move on with God until we heal. We first have to want this for ourselves. Some of us have made the wounds a part of our identity, but God says you are not a victim any longer. You are a survivor first, then a conqueror, and even more than a conqueror through Him who loves you (Romans 8:37).

Through a revelation of God's love for us, we can get inner healing for all our hurts. There are those who specialize in this type of ministry. Please seek them out and get your healing. If you're not sure where you need healing or what thoughts hold you captive, God can reveal it to you. Pray the prayer King David prayed in Psalm 139:23-24 (NLT).

Search me, O God, and know my heart; test me and know my anxious thoughts. Point out anything in me that offends you, and lead me along the path of everlasting life.

Once we trust God with our hearts and minds, we are free to let Him work on our vessel. We are the vessel Jesus uses to carry something He gives us. We cannot go to Him full of something that isn't from Him. We must be empty.

Some of us are filled with unforgiveness. This means we have no room to receive God's forgiveness (Matthew 6:14). We all have wounds and sometimes we feel we need to hold onto them because we believe our wall protects us. However, we must forgive others before Jesus can fill our vessel.

Forgiveness has little to do with the people who hurt you. That's another lie of the enemy. He says, "Don't forgive them. They don't deserve it." His motive is to keep you from receiving your forgiveness. I don't know about you, but that makes me mad. I want God's forgiveness, and I don't want anything standing in the way.

I have discovered that I need to forgive myself for bad things I've done, said, and believed. If we hold onto those bad things, we reject God's forgiveness. If we think our sins aren't so bad, we diminish who God is and render Jesus's sacrifice meaningless. Then, even though we are repulsed by the bad, we elevate ourselves above God. We must empty ourselves of ourselves, dying to ourselves and denying ourselves (Luke 9:23).

If we think we aren't good enough, we are full of self-doubt and not fit to carry anything. Conversely, if we think we know how God should use us, then we are full of pride and not fit to carry anything. Do you see where thinking too much or too little of ourselves are both harmful to our walk? Thinking of ourselves at all is the problem and is self-centered. We must become God-centered instead. How do we do that? By allowing God to refine us.

God does that in two ways. The first is by separating the wheat from the chaff.

His winnowing fork is in his hand, and he will clear his threshing floor, gathering his wheat into the barn and burning up the chaff with unquenchable fire (Matthew 3:12).

In the wheat plant, the chaff surrounds the seed. The seed is good and we plant it. But the chaff is refuse, waste, garbage, debris, or scrap. We have both good seed and garbage in our lives. We need to allow God to separate those things, keeping what is good and burning what is scrap. Giving God access to our lives and allowing Him to take away what is unacceptable is another form of surrender that cleans our vessel.

Do you remember when I said I had just lost a lot of weight? That was a result of God separating the wheat from the chaff. He wanted to show me things in my character that needed to be removed—overindulgence and a lack of self-control. I could not move on in the Spirit until my vessel was empty of these things. Praise the Lord that the emptying also resulted in a brand-new outer vessel.

Refine them as silver is refined, and test them as gold is tested. They will call on My name, and I will answer them; I will say, "They are My people," and they will say, "The Lord is my God" (Zechariah 13:9 NASB).

Another way He refines us is similar to the refining process of fine metals like silver and gold. In the refining process, the refiner puts metal into a pot and heats it to extreme temperatures until the metal melts. As it melts, impurities rise to the surface, and the refiner skims them off. When all the impurities are removed, only the precious metal remains.

God refines us with fire. This comes in the form of tests, trials, and hardships. When He does this, we often feel we've done something wrong rather than seeing it as God's favor toward us. He releases just the right amount of heat and pressure to the right events to bring the needed change and healing through these tests.

Suffering can reveal a lot about us. It shows us what we're made of. Do we back down or rise to the occasion? We never know until we're put to the test. Have you ever wondered why you keep running into the same problem? In the past, when a problem presented itself, I used manipulation to get the outcome I wanted. I thought I had such good, creative ideas. But when they all failed, I wondered where I'd gone wrong. I was disappointed many times.

But then God revealed that I didn't trust Him with the outcome, and I was manipulating the situation. Every time I manipulated, I voided God's provision and blessing, which I wanted and He wanted to give. The next time a problem arose, so did my instinct to manipulate. It was difficult to let the outcome rest with God. Each time got a little easier as He developed in me the ability to trust Him more and me less.

Each time we face problems, He skims impurities from us, leaving us better equipped to face the next problem. He loves you just as you are, but He doesn't leave you where you are. Let's take a look at someone in the Bible whom God was not going to leave as he was. Jacob's name means deceiver. You can read about Jacob's life in the chapters of Genesis 27-35. He had deceived everyone everywhere he went. He deceived Esau out of his birthright, and he deceived Laban in order to get his cattle. He had lived up to his name. No matter how far he traveled, he could not escape who he was. Not until he decided to let everything go, and he was all alone with himself, did God meet him right where he was.

God sent an angel to wrestle with him. I don't know of anyone who hasn't wrestled with God in his heart and mind in order to change. But in the end, God touched Jacob and transformed him. In fact, He gave him a new name, Israel. That name means God contends or "fights for." It's the name of God's chosen people whom he has fought for throughout history. And, since we are also chosen by God through Jesus, He fights for us as well. It was only when Jacob let go of the things of this world that he was in a position for God to touch him. And that touch transformed him from who he was into who God meant for him to be. God changes us, transforming us into who He means for us to be, and that is into the image of His son.

God doesn't stop His refining work until all impurities are removed and only the gold remains within us. This is a lifelong process, but one day, God promises we will reflect the image of Jesus.

So all of us who have had that veil removed can see and re-flect the glory of the Lord. And the Lord—who is the Spirit—makes us more and more like him as we are changed into his glorious image (2 Corinthians 3:18 NLT).

Thoughts on Layer One

Many Christians never go deeper than Layer One, choosing to spend their lives in shallow waters. They refuse to surrender, instead holding onto worries as they try to maintain control. They resist the healing and refining process because it's difficult and painful.

Let me encourage you. Jesus did all this. He is our example. He quickly moved through the process, showing us how to walk in obedience, surrendered to the Father. He was not spared the suffering, but God promises that, if we share in His suffering, we will also share in His resurrection power. This suffering might be hard to go through now, but will be worth it for the rest of our lives. Allowing God to bring healing and growth not only brings Him glory, but it also brings our eternal change and blessing. We must share the sentiment Paul expressed when he wrote to the Philippians:

I want to know Christ—yes, to know the power of his resurrection and participation in his sufferings, becoming like him in death (Philippians 3:10).

Layer One is all about participating in Christ's sufferings in order to die to self. Most Christians think this is the only part of their growth process in Christ. But there is more.

Do you want to know about the power that resurrected Christ from the dead? Do you want to identify with and participate in that? Well, then let's go a little deeper.

Discussion Questions

1. What things can you now see are idols in your life? What are some practical ways you can dethrone them?

2. What is your initial response to the word "surrender"? How does the world view this word? How do you think surrendering to God is different?

3. What do you think of the analogy of the censer?

4. What do your prayers currently look like? How are they similar to the example prayer, and how are they different?

5. What walls have you put around your heart? What walls have you put around your mind? What event in your life might have led you to build those walls?

6. Can you identify an area in your life that God is refining? What problem does He continually allow you to face?

7. What impurities might God be trying to skim from your life?

8. What did you identify with most in this layer? Do you struggle to understand anything in this layer?

Layer Two

BUILDING A FIRM FOUNDATION AND RECEIVING THE FULL MEASURE

⸙ Seven ⸙

TEMPLE: A CONTINUAL FILLING
OF HIS HOLY SPIRIT

And the train of his robe filled the temple (Isaiah 6:1 BSB).

Once we put God in His rightful place and see Him seated on the throne, He fills us. We've died to self; our vessels are empty. We are in the right condition for God to fill us with His Holy Spirit. The word "filled" in this verse is one of continual filling. The train of God's robe is not finite. No, it comes in and keeps on coming—a continual filling—just as the Holy Spirit's filling is not a one time event; it too is continual. This is different than receiving the Holy Spirit at conversion. At conversion, you are given the Holy Spirit as a guarantee of your inheritance (Ephesians 1:14) and as a seal or mark of ownership (2 Corinthians 1:22).

We need to seek and ask for this continual filling of the Holy Spirit. As we pour ourselves out, the Lord draws us back to the well for another filling. As you go out from the well, you carry the Holy Spirit with you. When you pour out or release Him, you come back to the well for more. You will not have a continual filling if you do not return to the well. Your vessel will run dry.

When Jesus fed the multitudes with only two fish and five loaves (Matthew 14:13-21), He gave the food to the disciples. As they handed it out, the food multiplied, and their baskets continually filled. When they had finished, they returned to Jesus. This is what we must remember to do.

Also notice the leftover food. God fills us to overflowing (Proverbs 3:10). He gives with an abundant, overflowing measure. We must seek this type of filling. Nothing but an overabundance of the Holy Spirit will do. With a continual, overflowing filling of the Holy Spirit, we can accomplish all God has called us to do.

And God is able to bless you abundantly, so that in all things at all times, having all that you need, you will abound in every good work (2 Corinthians 9:8).

One thing that holds us back from accomplishing our calling is insecurity. We still see ourselves as the "old me," so we focus on our faults and shortcomings. However, God says we are a new creation. We are not the same as we once were. Not only are our vessels empty, but He is shaping our vessels into something completely new. We must be like jars of clay, molded by the hands of the Potter (2 Corinthians 4:7). After He molds us, we will never be the same. The person you were before is dead, and you are now alive in Christ (Romans 6:11).

Therefore if anyone is in Christ, he is a new creation. The old has passed away. Behold, the new has come! (2 Corinthians 5:17 ESV)

I like the word "behold" in this translation. It implies a masterpiece has just been created. No matter how much your sin tarnished your old vessel, your new vessel is something to behold. This is another reason we must return to the well. While we sit in His presence, God tells us who we are, a little at a time, so we can grasp how wide and long and high and deep is the love of Christ (Ephesians 3:14-21). In His presence, a love story plays out, strengthening you in your identity as He tells you that you belong to Him and reveals the wonderful thoughts He thinks about you.

Once, while I sat in His presence, He gave me a revelation of a peeled onion. We've probably all heard the analogy of God peeling away our layers as we would peel an onion. On this occasion, He had just peeled a layer from me, and I saw myself naked and cold. Then I saw Him put a robe on me. Festal robes in the Bible (Zechariah 3:4 NASB) often have to do with taking off our dirty clothes and putting on pure, clean, or white clothing. The Lord told me that every time He takes something off, He replaces it with a new, clean robe. In this case, I received a robe of victory. As God changes us, He gives us an upgrade: His robe of righteousness. He replaces our filthy garments with garments fit for a high priest or a bride.

> *I will greatly rejoice in the Lord; my soul shall exult in my God, for he has clothed me with the garments of salvation; he has covered me with the robe of righteousness, as a bridegroom decks himself like a priest with a beautiful headdress, and as a bride adorns herself with her jewels* (Isaiah 61:10 ESV).

We need to start believing we are who God says we are and seeing ourselves as He sees us. Old Testament priests had to wash in the bronze basin before they could enter the temple's Holy Place. As they washed, they looked at their reflection in the basin. As God begins to cleanse us, we see the reflection of Jesus as we become more like Him. Knowing our identity in Christ gives us confidence to do what God calls us to do and to become the one God has called us to be.

~ Eight ~

WORSHIP: OFFERING PRAISE AND THANKSGIVING WHILE STANDING ON THE WORD

Enter his gates with thanksgiving and his courts with praise; give thanks to him and praise his name (Psalm 100:4).

In biblical times, if you wanted to make a request of the king, you first had to get in the door (the gate), then you entered his court (the throne room where he sits with his subjects). No one could go before the king without his permission. If they did, they could be put to death.

Queen Esther risked her life when she went before King Xerxes without an appointment. She had a huge request, so she put on her royal robes and entered his court, according to the book of Esther. I think she put on her royal robes not only to remind the king who she was, but also to remind herself. When she entered the king's court, he recognized her and extended his scepter to her.

When we come into God's courts, we need to know who we are. We too are royalty because we are His children. In right standing with God, we wear His robe of righteousness. Our thanksgiving gets us in the door, and once in His courts, we praise His name. Then He turns His face toward us, recognizes us as His child, and gives us His attention. He extends His scepter to us and says, "What is your request?"

When Queen Esther reached this point, she said, "If I have found favor with the king, and if it pleases the king to grant my request and do what I ask." As with Esther, our thanksgiving and praise gives us great favor with the King, stirring in Him the desire to give you what you ask. In this position, you can pray for anything, and if you believe you've received it, it will be yours (Mark 11:24 NLT).

God is enthroned upon our praises (Psalm 22:3). This means God inhabits our praises. It means He sits and remains seated to inhabit and dwell. When we get into His presence, we are to remain and dwell in His presence while He ministers to us. Can you imagine the God of the universe enjoying your worship so much that He wants to dwell there? What a beautiful picture!

One of the best ways to get into His presence is to worship. As you worship, He inhabits you. You remain; He remains. This mutual habitation is intimacy at its highest level: you in Him and He in you. This cohabitation is called communing with God. That is where we get the term "communion," which means "common union." You are communing with or having a common union with Jesus in that moment of receiving the elements of the bread and wine. You take within you the body and blood of Christ, creating a state in which He is in you. Your remembrance of Him places you in Him, establishing an intimate habitation. From this place of communion, you are aligned with Jesus, receiving the benefits of His life and partaking of His divine nature. Both taking communion and communing with Him in worship put you in this state of co-habitation.

His throne is also a place of judgment and decision. Through our thanksgiving and praise, He seats himself in a place to bring judgment on your prayer and render a decision. If you are praying with the right motives, the judgment will be in your favor.

> *And we are confident that he hears us whenever we ask for anything that pleases Him. And since we know he hears us when we make our requests, we also know that he will give us what we ask for* (1 John 5:14-15 NLT).

When you make a request of God, what do you ask for? Are your prayers specific or general? Are they bold or timid? I encourage you to take advantage of your position and ask with confidence. Now is not the time to remind God of all your problems. He already knows. Now is the time to remind God of His promises. He also knows the promises in His Word, and when He hears you speak them back to Him, He releases creative life and power in that Word. His Word always accomplishes what He wants it to accomplish. And you don't have to wonder whether His Word is His will for you. It is already written. Therefore, it is His will.

> *It is the same with my word. I send it out, and it always produces fruit. It will accomplish all I want it to, and it will prosper everywhere I send it* (Isaiah 55:11 NLT).

So again, what are you asking for? We've established that

His promises are "yes and amen" (2 Corinthians 1:20), and if you ask and believe, it is yours. How big are you believing? Maybe your asking is small because your belief is small. I challenge you today to expand your capacity to believe. If your vessel is a sixteen-ounce water bottle, your capacity to hold water is only sixteen ounces, and all you will ever receive is sixteen ounces. You can increase what you receive by increasing the size of your vessel. Determine today to be a thirty-two ounce Big Gulp. Better yet, a ten-gallon bucket.

For the longest time, my prayer life resembled begging. My capacity to believe that God would hear me, let alone answer me, was pretty small. In fact, it was the size of a thimble. One day, I lost the diamond in my anniversary ring. In a panic, I looked everywhere. First, I retraced my steps in the grocery store and the parking lot. While I looked through my car and the trash, I realized I needed to call in the big guns—my prayer-warrior friends. God would surely hear them.

Then I had a new thought: I'm going to believe God for this. He is going to help me find my diamond.

I began to pray. I began to tell him how big He was and how nothing is impossible for Him; in fact, with God, all things are possible. Then came the bold question: "God, will you put my diamond in the middle of my floor where it is obvious and I can find it? I am tired of looking."

I went upstairs to my daughter's nursery to sit in the rocker and rest because I was exhausted. There I spotted something in the middle of the floor, nestled in the carpet under the ceiling fan. I bent down. It was my diamond!

In that moment, I went from the thimble to the Big Gulp. For the first time in my life, I knew God was real and that He'd heard me. Not only did He hear me, but He loved me enough to answer my prayer. Awestruck, I fell on my face and worshipped Him.

It's amazing to realize God knows you. My capacity to believe grew that day. I now carry the knowledge that belief is powerful; His Word is powerful. Do you know His Word?

Knowing His promises is the key to praying His promises. You will find them in the Bible. If you need God's help, get in His Word and find out what He has already said about your situation. The Bible contains the promise that is the answer to your situation. When wielded by a believing heart, the promise produces results.

But many of us don't know the Word. We need to open the Word every day and memorize His promises. Knowing only part of a verse is like fighting with a broken sword. The Word of God is rightfully called the Sword of the Spirit (Ephesians 6:17). It must be fully forged in order to be effective. We must speak it and pray it out loud; then God will release its power. When we do this in faith, God changes our situation and brings our perceived reality into alignment with heaven's reality.

Your Word, O Lord, is eternal; it stands firm in the heavens (Psalm 119:89 NLT).

An important aspect of speaking God's Word is believing it. We must come into agreement with it through faith and through the words that we use everyday. The Bible says that life and death is in the power of our tongue (Proverbs 18:21). Yes, our words have power. We have the power to speak life or death over a situation, over ourselves, and over others just by the words we choose to speak. Even the smallest word spoken matters. Look what it says in Matthew12:36-37.

*And I tell you this, you must give an account on judgement day for **every idle word** you speak. The words you say will either acquit you or condemn you* (author emphasis).

Look at the words "acquit or condemn." They mean life or death. Both blessings and curses come out of our mouths, so we must learn, by the power of the Holy Spirit, to tame our tongue as James 3:1-10 suggests. How do we do this? It's starts with examining what's in our hearts. Out of the abundance of the heart, the mouth speaks (Luke 6:45). Therefore, above all else, we must guard our heart. Proverbs 4:23-27 says that everything we do and say flows through it. We must be careful what influences us. Friends, what you let in through your eyes and ears, gets into your mind and heart and is what eventually comes out of your mouth and moves your feet. Pay attention to what you are talking about. It is an indication of what you believe and is what will guide your actions. Are those beliefs and actions lining up with God or lining up with the enemy? For example, have you or someone you loved gotten a bad diagnosis? Who's report have you believed, the doctor's or God's?

When my sister got sick, I was just beginning to learn to stand on His Word. She went in for a routine laparoscopic surgery. While she was in surgery, I was reading the Bible and came across a verse that said, "He is before all things, and in Him all things hold together" (Colossians 1:17). It was highlighted by the Lord to me for my sister. I began to pray that. Well, her surgery took a very bad turn, and they had to open her up. She was in there for three hours when the doctor came out and told us it didn't look good. He said,

"Her tissue is just not holding together." Those were his words. However, I had just gotten a different word from the Lord. I began to encourage everyone that it would hold together because in Jesus, all things hold together. What I want you to first see is how God gave me that verse before I even knew I would need it. That's how He works. And He provided His healing first over two thousand years ago before any of us would need it. So take heart, the Word says, "Surely He took up our infirmities (sickness and disease) and by His stripes we are healed" (Isaiah 53:4-5), and Jesus said on the cross, "It is finished" (John 19:30). And in response, God said, "It is done" (Revelation 16:17), so what is it that you say? What we say matters. Adding what we say to what God has said will expand our belief and increase our faith faster than anything else because it is an equation that holds power—the power to overcome the enemy—and he knows it.

And they have conquered him by the blood of the Lamb and by the word of their testimony. . . (Revelation 12:11).

The Censer

In Layer Two, we are no longer a bronze censer. We are an empty censer, just as we are empty vessels, waiting for God to fill us with new fire. This is no longer a sacrificial fire, but the fire of His Word. When the incense (our prayers) is sprinkled onto the fire of His Word, smoke rises to the throne room with a familiarity that pleases the Lord. First, He recognizes us because we praise Him while wearing the robe of His righteousness. Then He recognizes us because our prayers carry His words. In this layer, we must see the importance of emptying our prayers of our own words and filling them with God's Word. Declare and decree His promises.

How should our prayers look in this layer? After inviting the Holy Spirit to come, check to see if anything is bothering you or distracting you. If so, release it to God as described in Layer One. We must always do this first to assure effectiveness when we declare and decree. Then thank Him for everything you are thankful for, and praise His name. Praise Him for who He is and what He does. As you do this, more will come to mind.

If you have trouble thinking of things to thank Him for, ask yourself this question: "What if I woke up tomorrow with only what I thanked Him for today?" Then state your situation and declare His promise over it. For example, your situation might be health related. You might say something like this: "Lord, I am suffering with this terrible cold. I know sickness is not your will, for your word says You took up our infirmities and carried our sorrows. It also says, 'By your wounds I am healed,' and 'Your word stands firm in the heavens.' I declare wholeness to come into my body in the name of Jesus."

Your situation might be financial. You might pray,

Lord, I'm struggling to pay my bills this month, but I know You are my Provider. My God shall supply all my needs according to His riches in glory by Christ Jesus, and He will rebuke the devourer for me, so he will not destroy the fruit of my labor. God, I claim Your promise from Deuteronomy, which says You will guarantee a blessing over everything I do, and You will fill my storehouses. You will give me prosperity in the land You promised me, and I declare that I am the top and not the bottom, the head and not the tail.

End by thanking Him for what He is doing or providing, and then believe it is done. When doubt creeps in, speak these same promises out loud to remind yourself of God's faithfulness. Your faith will begin to rise, enlarging your capacity to believe. "So then faith comes by hearing, and hearing by the word of God" (Romans 10:17 NKJV). Yes, even hearing God's Word coming from your own mouth will strengthen your faith. Finally, sit in silence and listen for God to speak to you. When you feel a release in your spirit, say, "Amen."

Nine

WALL: REBUILDING MY IDENTITY

But you are a chosen people, a royal priesthood, a holy nation, God's special possession, that you may declare the praises of Him who called you out of darkness into this wonderful light (1 Peter 2:9).

With all our walls dismantled, we may feel exposed and unprotected. We need to reestablish ourselves, but this time, let's allow God to establish us.

As He tells us who we are, He builds our identity on a firm foundation—the foundation that is the Rock; Jesus, the Word made flesh. He is the One who is the Way, the Truth, and the Life (John 14:16). Friends, you would be wise to establish your identity from the Word of God.

Everyone then who hears these words of mine and does them will be like a wise man who built his house on the rock (Matthew 7:24).

When you build on anything other than the rock, it is as foolish as building on sand. And the parable in Matthew tells us that when hard times come, your house will fall (Matthew 7:25-26). You can stand when your feet are on solid ground. Sand shifts beneath your feet. One day you feel you are capable, and another day you feel inadequate. These feelings are founded on your circumstances, which are ever changing. God's Word says that you are in right standing no matter what circumstances you may be facing. You must believe the whole Bible. The entire Bible is the Rock, not just a few verses. Picking a few verses to believe is also like sand. A few verses will not establish you because someone can always come along and challenge that verse, but the whole Bible, where Jesus is revealed throughout, cannot be disputed. It becomes a banner of truth that can be held above your life, and who God says you are can become a shield that can be put over your heart.

This foundation of truth and love comes only from a loving Heavenly Father who created and knows the real us. Read from Psalm 139 and feel how much the Father loves you:

> *For you formed my inward parts; you knitted me together in my mother's womb. I praise you, for I am fearfully and wonderfully made. Wonderful are your works; my soul knows it very well. My frame was not hidden from you, when I was being made in secret, intricately. Woven in the depths of the earth. Your eyes saw my unformed substance; in your book were written, every one of them, the days that were formed for me, when as yet there was none of them* (Psalm 139:13-16).

The Lord knows us better than a mother knows the baby growing in her womb. When God fills us with the Holy

Spirit, He testifies with our spirit that we are God's children (Romans 8:16). He is the King of kings, which makes us royalty—sons and daughters of the Most High God.

And since we are his children, we are his heirs. In fact, together with Christ we are heirs of God's glory (Romans 8:17 NLT).

He also knows us like an artist knows his work. Only the artist knows the depth, purpose, and potential of his creation. Others may try to interpret, define, or categorize it, but they would only be guessing. Even the creation itself does not know its real purpose without the creator (Isaiah 45:9). One of the things God puts in our hearts when He created us was eternity and Himself.

Yet God has made everything beautiful for its own time. He has planted eternity in the human heart, but even so, people cannot see the whole scope of God's work from beginning to end (Ecclesiastes 3:11 author emphasis).

In John 17:3, Jesus defines eternal life as knowing God. The word "knowing" refers to an intimate knowledge, not just head knowledge. It is the type of knowing that can only come from having a relationship with and experiencing Him. It is during this "time" that the beauty of who we are and our purpose is revealed.

A few years ago a new song called "Oceans" was released by Hillsong United. When I sang along with that song, I would always just weep and weep. It was a good song, but this kind of response could only be the working of the Holy

Spirit. Little did I know that as I sang that song, my heart was actually crying out from somewhere deep within me. "Take me deeper" became a prayer released as I sang that song. It was a prayer that the Creator already put inside me, when He knit me together in my mother's womb, which was revealed "for its own time." This time, for such a time as this, it would be part of my purpose.

When we embrace this new identity and see ourselves as God sees us, we can walk in the covering, victory, and authority of the finished work of the cross. We must stop seeing ourselves as sinners, but dead to sin and alive in Christ (Romans 6:11). This is where we stop identifying with the "old rugged cross" and start identifying with Christ's "cross of victory." We have died to self and to sin, no longer bound by the flesh or its desires.

When we are tempted, Jesus presents a way out: His blood, which covers us. His shed blood is the ultimate act of love (John 15:13). Love covers a multitude of sins (1 Peter 4:8). Why is it important to be covered by the blood? Let's say you and some friends were out playing and you all fell in a mud puddle, and you're covered in mud. You run home to tell your father what happened and that your friends are coming over to get cleaned up. He says, "How will I know they are your friends?" You say, "Father, my friends are covered with mud from head to toe. They look just like me."

When God looks at you, He does not see your sin. He sees you covered in the blood of Jesus (Romans 5:9 NLT). You look just like Him, so He sees His son. This is the third way God recognizes you.

Now let's say you and those same friends are going to a concert. You arrive first and pay the way for the rest of your friends, and you go inside to the concert. Your friends arrive later and discover they have no money to get in. Nothing they do will gain them entrance. Then you come out and remind the employee at the door that you paid their way. You paid the price, and they are covered. Being covered by the blood of Jesus tells the Father we belong to Jesus, and we know He paid the price for us. He made a way for us to enter, and we come in only by the blood of Jesus. We need to understand that His blood redeemed and cleansed us, made us righteous, justified us, provided forgiveness, and made us clean (Ephesians 1:7).

> *For God knew his people in advance, and he chose them to become like his Son, so that his Son would be the firstborn among many brothers and sisters. And having chosen them, he called them to come to him. And having called them, he gave them right standing with himself. And having given them right standing, he gave them his glory* (Romans 8:29-30 NLT).

When Jesus died on the cross, a divine exchange took place: everything we are for everything He is. Think about that. He exchanged His life for ours. He took our place, taking upon Himself all our iniquities, infirmities, transgressions, sorrows, and the judgment that was rightfully ours (Isaiah 53:4-9 BSB). Then He gave us His righteousness, sonship, His authority, and His victory. When the Father looks at us, He sees Jesus. We have "Christ in us, the hope of Glory" (Colossians 1:27). He lives through us.

In his book, *Hosting the Presence,* Bill Johnson says God doesn't cancel out who we are, but He captures who we are to the fullest. He immerses us in His divine influence, so our personality and demeanor are expressed through the filter of God living in us, revealing yet more of His glory. Because of this, our foundation and identity are established. With God's Word on our hearts and in our mouths, we are surely protected, just as David was protected when he fought the Philistine giant, Goliath.

David knew who he was when he fought Goliath. He never could have done that without first being secure in his identity. We can't move on to Layer Three until we understand this principle, which David understood as a youth. How did David know who He was? First, he knew his heritage. Second, he knew his history with God.

David was from the tribe of Judah. The Philistines camped their army in Judah, and David knew this land was his inheritance, promised by God. He also knew his people were a chosen people, and God had performed many miracles and led them to victory through the generations. So he knew where he came from.

He also knew where he was going. Just a short time before this, Samuel the prophet had anointed David the next king of Israel. You can read more of these accounts in 1 Samuel chapters sixteen and seventeen. David had a history with God, since he was with Him on the hillsides while he tended his sheep. Also, while on that hillside, David had encountered and conquered both a bear and a lion. What you do in private prepares you for what God will have you do in public. Private battles are won long before public battles arise. This established David's history with God, just as finding my diamond established my history with God and revealed more of His glory as I released great faith.

Every shepherd carried a staff. They often carved images of significant events on them. David probably had engraved pictures of his victories over the bear and the lion on his staff, and he saw them when he picked up his staff and sling to go into battle against the giant. He had all he needed. You can hear in his speech to Goliath (1 Samuel 17:45-47) that he had more than a sling and five stones. He had his identity, his heritage, and his history with God when he stretched out his arm and flung that rock with everything he was. God's glory was revealed as David exercised his great faith.

Thoughts on Layer Two

Do you know who you are? Spend some time understanding your heritage and inheritance in Christ. Review your history with God. Journal your faith stories so you can draw upon them regularly. Once you embrace your heritage and history, it no longer becomes about where you've been but where you're headed. Following by faith is a great adventure!

Did you know the name Judah means "praise"? This name not only established David in who he was, but also who he would become. David was a talented musician and wrote most of the Psalms. He also ushered in a new way to serve and please God, a way that didn't involve sacrifice but became the prototype of the New Testament church: worship.

Who will you become? God wants to dream and plan with you in His presence. Bill Johnson points out that we should pay attention to our desires and passions when we're in prayer. When we get into God's presence, He brings life to them and builds upon them. He downloads His desires into you so your desires will line up with His. "Delight yourself in the Lord, He shall give you the desires of your heart" (Psalm

37:4). God allows us to dream, plan, and create with Him. These desires become part of what the Holy Spirit gives you to carry.

Layer Two is all about learning to become a worshiper and learning our identity. Once we know who we are in Christ, and we are armed with His Word, we can partner with what He's doing in the earth. We can also come against the enemy and what he's doing in the earth. We can co-labor with the Trinity to advance the kingdom of God. Does this sound exciting? If so, then it's time to go deeper.

Discussion Questions

1. How is your prayer life, now that you've put into practice some of the prayer principles from Layer One? What differences do you notice?

2. Describe the difference between being filled at conversion and receiving a continual filling.

3. In what ways is God molding you? What things still need to be emptied out of your vessel?

4. Are thanksgiving and praise part of your prayer life? Does it come easy to you, or do you find it difficult or uncomfortable? What is your understanding of it now?

5. Do you read your Bible on a regular basis? Have you tried to memorize Scripture? If so, what was the result? How do you now understand the value of this practice?

6. What is your capacity to believe? Does the idea of asking big or declaring God's promises make you uncomfortable? Why or why not?

7. What spoke most to you about establishing your identity in Christ? Why do you think it's important to know who you are in Christ?

8. What did you identify with most in this layer? Is there anything you still struggle to understand in this layer?

Layer Three

AWAKENING TO AUTHORITY AND RELEASING HIS POWER

≈ *Ten* ≈

TEMPLE: THE HOLY SPIRIT RESTS ON ME LIKE A DOVE AS I YIELD TO HIM

And when Jesus was baptized, immediately he went up from the water, and behold, the heavens were opened to him, and he saw the Spirit of God descending like a dove and coming to rest on him (Matthew 3:16 ESV).

After we are baptized in the Holy Spirit, the Spirit is both in us and upon us. As Bill Johnson writes in his book, *Hosting the Presence,* "He is in us for us, but He is upon us for others." This is what Jesus meant when He said in Isaiah 61:1, "The Spirit of the Sovereign Lord is upon me, He has anointed me to bring good news to the poor. He has sent me to comfort the broken-hearted."

Here we understand that Jesus was the Anointed One or the Sent One. God wants to anoint and send us to do the same things (preach, comfort, bind, and proclaim). But we must be baptized with the Holy Spirit. This baptism is different than water baptism. It is not a decision we make; rather, Jesus gives it to us.

We must understand this separate baptism of the Holy

Spirit if we are to operate under His anointing. *The New Living Translation* of John 14:17 speaks of the Holy Spirit and clarifies this by saying, "The world cannot receive Him, because it isn't looking for Him and doesn't recognize Him. But you know Him, because He lives with you now and later will be in you." There are two baptisms, and we need to look for Him. We receive the baptism of the Holy Spirit when we are seeking it in prayer. The key to receiving is asking.

> *Ask, and it shall be given you; seek, and you shall find; knock, and it shall be opened to you. For everyone that asks receives; and he that seeks finds; and to him that knocks it shall be opened. If a son shall ask bread of any of you that is a father, will he give him a stone? Or if he ask a fish, will he for a fish give him a serpent? Or if he shall ask an egg, will he offer him a scorpion? If you then, being evil, know how to give good gifts to your children: how much more shall your heavenly Father give the Holy Spirit to them that ask him?* (Luke 11:9-13 NKJV)

We sometimes mistakenly use these verses to ask for blessings, thinking that if we ask God for good things, He won't give us bad things instead. Did you ever think the last verse was odd? What does the Holy Spirit have to do with asking for blessings?

The truth is, this is our directive to ask for the Holy Spirit. The previous verses (Luke 11:5-8) teach us about persistence. When we are persistent in seeking and asking for the baptism of the Holy Spirit, God promises to give it. After we've received, we can ask for even more of the Holy Spirit because it's a continual filling, not a one-time event. If we don't continually ask and seek, we limit our receiving.

We can receive the baptism of the Holy Spirit at the same time as water baptism, but many times God gives it at a different time. They are two separate baptisms, but God decides when to baptize us with His Holy Spirit. Jesus will send Him when we are ready to receive Him.

> *I baptize you with water for repentance. But after me comes one who is more powerful than I. . . He will baptize you with the Holy Spirit and fire* (Matthew 3:11).

We also need to look for Him after our baptism in the Holy Spirit. Pray and ask God to make His presence known. In the beginning I would pray, "Lord, let me feel Your presence. Let me be more and more aware of You." And that's exactly what He did. When He comes to rest upon us, He will make it known in some way, but we may not recognize it. We have to train our senses to be aware of the quickening of the Holy Spirit. Sometimes it can be so dramatic that you know something is different. Other times it's subtle and we can miss it. The first things I noticed were tears and then a lump in my throat. I thought it was natural to have a lump in my throat, since I was crying. I missed its meaning for a long time. Then I noticed the lump in my throat without the tears. First, I didn't recognize the tears as the work of the Holy Spirit, and second, the lump was His presence. Once I acknowledged His presence, He began to show me other ways He was upon me.

I'll never forget the first time I got "the tingles." I was praying and soaking with my friend Katie when I felt a tingling sensation in my hands and the bottoms of my feet. I didn't know what was happening, but I thought I could possibly pass them on to Katie. So we sat facing each other, hand to hand and feet to feet. It did not transfer, by the way. But the next morning, during my prayer time, I noticed the tingles again. I thought it was strange, and I wondered when it would go away while I hoped it wouldn't.

During another time of soaking (meditating on the Lord while listening to music), the tingles in my hands moved up my arms and from my feet to my legs. I thought I could make them meet in the middle, but they didn't. Also, I had a strange sensation in my head (a type of full heaviness). It felt like intoxication. On other occasions, the top of my head tingled. Sometimes it was so intense, I thought something would explode right out the top. Thankfully, nothing did.

Then one day the tingles subsided, and I didn't notice them as much. But I began to notice something new. When I prayed with my eyes closed, I saw colors dancing and blending in front of my mind's eye—first purple, then green. It is always the same two colors, but sometimes a light blue comes into the periphery. I tell you this because maybe something similar has happened to you, but you didn't think anything about it. Or maybe something completely different has happened, but again you never imagined it could be the Holy Spirit.

Once my grandmother told me about an annoying thing that happened to her from time to time, and she couldn't figure out what was going on. Something simple and completely natural was happening with regularity. Her eyes watered and then her nose ran. It wasn't because she was sad or had a cold. I explained that it could be the presence of the Holy Spirit. As we talked more about the Holy Spirit, I began to feel the tingles and sensed He was upon me. My grandmother began to tell me about a pain she had in her neck. Well, I knew He wanted to do something in that moment, so I began to pray for her. God healed my grandma's neck that day, and it has not bothered her since.

Is the Holy Spirit trying to get our attention, but we are not looking for Him? Start looking for Him today. If you seek Him, you will find Him.

The purpose of the Holy Spirit upon us is not necessarily to give us a physical experience, although it's nice when He does. No, this is the first step in becoming aware of Him and what He wants to do through you to help others. God wants to move us from focusing on ourselves to ministering to and blessing others. Only when we yield to the Holy Spirit can God work and act through us for His good purpose. As we sense what God is doing and yield to His promptings, the Holy Spirit will rest upon us and allow us to operate in the anointing so we can bless others, much like what He did for the apostles in Acts. They started out as frightened disciples, but after they received the Holy Spirit, they went around healing, teaching, preaching boldly, and testifying powerfully and great grace was upon them all (Acts 4:33). This grace is the favor of God and operational power of the Holy Spirit. He is the one who gives us something to carry.

We don't need to search for ways to serve God. Instead, we should look where He is already working. He is constantly at work, and when we tune in to that, He invites us to join Him. He doesn't need a bunch of Marthas doing chores He didn't ask us to do. No, He asks us to be like Mary and choose what is better (Luke 10:42). What is better is at the feet of Jesus, in the secret place of prayer. Let Him lead you, not the other way around. We need to be His ears and heart long before we can be His hands and feet. This is exactly how Jesus did it while on the earth.

> *My Father is always at his work to this very day, and I, too, am working. I tell you the truth, the Son can do nothing by himself; he can only do what he sees his Father doing, because whatever the Father does the Son also does. For the Father loves the Son and shows him all he does* (John 5:17,19-20).

Jesus is our model. He showed us how to live completely yielded to God, operating in the power of the Holy Spirit. Before He ascended to heaven, He commissioned us to do the same. Let's take a look at the Great Commission Jesus gave us as recorded in the book of Mark.

> *Go into all the world and preach the Good News to everyone. Anyone who believes and is baptized will be saved. But anyone who refuses to believe will be condemned. These miraculous signs will accompany those who believe: They will cast out demons in my name, and they will speak in new languages. They will be able to handle snakes with safety, and if they drink anything poisonous, it won't hurt them. They will be able to place their hands on the sick, and they will be healed* (Mark 16:15-18 NLT).

We can easily accept the part of the Great Commission that starts with preaching the Good News and ends with people being saved. We are not as comfortable with telling people they will be condemned if they do not believe, and we are even more uncomfortable with the miraculous signs displayed by those who believe.

Don't settle for a truncated Commission. We are called to do more than preach. Jesus demonstrated the Kingdom by first teaching then healing. And wherever the Apostles preached the gospel, signs and wonders followed (Acts 4:29-30, Acts 14:3, Acts 8:6, Romans 15:18-19). When God invites or asks us to do something, it will challenge us. We will enter into what Henry Blackaby, in his book, *Experiencing God,* calls a "crisis of belief." We will always question it because God wants us to step out of our comfort zone. When we reach this crisis, we have two options. We can refuse and stay where we are, thus limiting our experience of God, or we can expand our belief and step out in obedience and encounter the miraculous, wonder-working God.

Once while I was driving in my car, the Holy Spirit prompted me to go to my mother-in-law's house and deliver a message. He gave me the message, but of course I had no way of knowing if it would mean anything to her.

I did not want to do this. I delayed this assignment and went on about my errands. After the last one, I felt the prompting again. I thought it wouldn't hurt to stop by, so I went. She complained about arthritis pain in her knees, and I felt the Lord wanted me to pray for her. First I delivered the message He wanted me to give, and then I put my hands on her knees. My left hand tingled and grew warm, making me aware that the Holy Spirit was involved in this prayer. While I was praying, I felt something pop out of her knee. It startled me so much that I stopped praying to look at her knee and my hand. There was nothing there, but I had felt something. She felt it too, so she bent her knee. The pain was gone.

If I hadn't stepped out in obedience, willing to risk looking foolish, I wouldn't have had that experience, and my belief wouldn't have expanded. And perhaps my mother-in-law wouldn't have received her healing. Allowing the Holy Spirit to work through us is another way of revealing God's glory as He moves us from glory to glory. Jesus gives us this promise in His Word:

> *I tell you the truth, anyone who believes in me will do the same works I have done, and even greater works, because I am going to be with the Father. You can ask for anything in my name, and I will do it, so that the Son can bring glory to the Father* (John 14:12-13 NLT).

Before we can do greater works, we have to do the same works. When we ask for anything in Jesus' name and miraculous signs and wonders follow, the Father is glorified and the witness's belief expands. Participating in the Great Commission in its entirety, bringing truth through the Gospel, and demonstrating the Kingdom are convincing and undeniable evidence.

In Romans 15:16-19, Paul writes that he is a special messenger from Christ Jesus to bring the Good News. But they were convinced by the miraculous signs and wonders done by the power of the Holy Spirit. Some may think this was only for Jesus and the Apostles. Who are we to perform signs and wonders? I thought the same thing. But remember, it's the Holy Spirit working through you. He can work through you because you have authority. When you know who you are in Christ, you have authority to enforce the victory of the cross. Christ achieved victory on the cross so we could enforce it through our authority. Let's take a closer look at this authority by going back and following the transfer of the keys of ownership/authority.

Our first stop is in the beginning, at creation. God has all authority over His creation. He said, "Let there be," and there was, until He made human beings and transferred dominion over the earth to man.

> *Then God said, "Let us make human beings in our image, to be like us . . . Then God blessed them and said, "Be fruitful and multiply. Fill the earth and govern it. Reign over the fish in the sea, the birds in the sky, and all the animals that scurry along the ground"* (Genesis 1:26 NLT).

Once He created human beings, He turned over the authority to govern and reign the earth to humanity. Jack Hayford, Executive Editor of *New Spirit-Filled Life Bible*, states that through the two of them together (male and female), God intended to live and reveal Himself in the world. Through them God intended to manifest His character and authority (image), express His dominion over the earth, display His indisputable power over the works of darkness, and subdue His archenemy, Satan. God chose to delegate dominion on the earth to man. He gave man the keys at creation.

How did man lose this authority to reign over the earth? We don't have to go any further than the garden to see that man gave the keys to Satan. "The serpent was the shrewdest of all the wild animals the Lord God had made. Did God really say you must not eat the fruit from any of the trees in the garden?" (Genesis 3:1). Satan will always make you question what God says. That's why it's so important to know the Word. If you know the Word, you know what God says. Then the serpent said, "God knows that your eyes will be opened as soon as you eat it, and you will be like God" (Genesis 3:3). They were already like God! They were created in His image with His character and authority.

The second thing the enemy will do is to make you doubt your identity. Through disobedience, man lost his dominion. Then, separated from God, man also lost the "life power" essential to ruling God's kingdom. Man forfeited rule to the serpent, and dominion of the earth fell to Satan. But because of the cross, Jesus now holds the keys over death (Revelation 1:18) and therefore took back the authority.

Jesus said to His disciples, "All authority in heaven and on earth has been given to me" (Matthew 28:18). With the commissioning, He gave us authority to preach, heal, cast out demons, and subdue the work of the enemy through the power of the Holy Spirit (Luke 10:19, Matthew 10:7-8 BSB). We lost authority through disobedience, but through obedience to the Holy Spirit, we can operate in the same power that raised Jesus from the dead. Hear Paul's incredible prayer for all of us:

> *I also pray that you will understand the incredible greatness of God's power for us who believe him. This is the same mighty power that raised Christ from the dead and seated him in the place of honor at God's right hand in the heavenly realms. Now he is far above any ruler or authority or power or leader or anything else—not only in this world but also in the world to come. God has put all things under the authority of Christ and has made him*

head over all things for the benefit of the church. And the church is his body; it is made full and complete by Christ, who fills all things everywhere with himself (Ephesians 1:19-23 NLT)

We are His body. The church is to be filled with the Holy Spirit, represent Him to the world, and minister His life, love, and power. God's design for us has always been to represent Him in the earth. It's time to step into our authority as His image bearers.

Because as He is, so also are we in this world (1 John 4:17 ESV).

WORSHIP: WHOLEHEARTED WORSHIP AND INTERCESSION FOR OTHERS

David, wearing a linen ephod, danced before the Lord with all his might (2 Samuel 6:14 BSB).

Love prompts us to do crazy things. We don't care how we look, if we're making a fool of ourselves, or who's watching. We are not focused on those things. All we want is to get the attention of the object of our affection.

That's what David was doing when he danced before the Lord and in front of his kingdom, dressed only in his undergarments. When God is the object of our affection and we have the indwelling of the Holy Spirit, we can't help but worship Him with our whole hearts. Nothing else will do. I sing louder than I used to because now I don't care if the person next to me hears me. I want God to hear me. I raise my hands and stretch them toward the sky because I want to touch Him. I even dance in my row and don't care if I accidentally bump the person to my right or left. I sing my own song between the songs. I never would have done that before.

When your love so overflows for God, you stop thinking

about your dignity and decorum. Worship will always look foolish to those who are not a part of the worship. They're there for entertainment. But your extravagant worship is a type of intercession for those on the fringes or just looking on. Isaiah 62:10 tells us:

> *Go through, go through the gates, clear the way for the people; Build up, build up the highway. Remove the stones, lift up a standard over the peoples* (Isaiah 62:10 ESV).

We go through the gates by way of worship. As we do, we clear the way for ourselves and others. Our wholehearted worship builds not just a path for one but also a highway where many can travel. This becomes the standard for worship for the people.

Then someone does something new, and the standard is raised. A new highway ushers in a new level of worship. When we're trying to break through or when we need a breakthrough, we sometimes have to do something we've never done before. If you do only what you've always done, you'll get only what you've always gotten. Step out, do something new, and get your breakthrough. If you've never raised your hands, then raise them. If you've never fallen on your knees, then get down. If you've never fasted, then fast. Whatever it is, purpose to do it. Obey whatever God prompts you to do. Obey!

I was once in a prayer and worship service in which the worship leader told us to worship God in a new way. At first, I didn't know what that might be. Then I felt I was to get low. So I knelt down, put my face to the carpet, and worshipped. Then, before I knew it, I was sobbing (you know, ugly crying with snot and everything). The Holy Spirit was lowering the walls around my heart. The natural outcome was to release my feelings in heartfelt sobs. I blessed what God was doing and gave thanks that I got low because I left there renewed.

Sometimes doing a new thing means singing a new song.

Sing a new song to the Lord! Let the whole earth sing to the Lord! Sing to the Lord; praise his name. Each day proclaim the good news that he saves (Psalm 96:1-2 NLT).

Sometimes we get stuck in a routine of prayer, songs, or even praise. Our routine can lead us into stagnation. This keeps us stuck on one plane instead of setting a new standard or building the highway higher. We need to see God new and fresh every day.

During a change of the seasons, we look out the window one day and notice the leaves have changed to vibrant colors or the buds on the trees have become green leaves overnight. We need a similar experience with God every day. Look out the window of your life and see God afresh. See the new thing He is doing! His mercies are new every morning (Lamentations 3:23-24 ESV). We must have a new vision of God, a new way to praise Him, and a new song to sing to Him.

Do you experience Him anew every day? Our desire should be to get into His presence every morning. Each day, He can show us something new, give us a new glimpse of who He is. We need to stay connected to the Vine. The book of John tells us to remain in Him. Jesus promises to remain in us (John 15:4).

Yes, I am the vine; you are the branches. Those who re-main in me, and I in them will produce much fruit. For apart from me you can do nothing (John 15:5 NLT).

Being in God's presence teaches us dependence on Him. If we get out of His presence and begin to operate outside the Spirit, our efforts won't produce fruit. We can try all we want in our own abilities and strength, but we will tire ourselves out. We need to be connected to Him so His "life sap" flows through us. Just as sap flows from a vine to its branches, so the Holy Spirit flows to us. Attached to the vine, we allow the invisible spiritual life to flow. When we're connected in this way and we remain in Him and His words remain in us, we may ask for anything we want, and He will grant it (John 15:7).

This is the perfect position to ask not only for ourselves, but to bring someone else's needs before God as well. "Carry each other's burdens, and in this way you will fulfill the law of Christ" (Galatians 6:2). What is the law of Christ? To love our neighbor as ourselves (Mark 12:31). Christ did every-thing out of love and compassion for the people. He saw their great burden and had compassion for them. In intercession, we carry the weight of another person's burden into God's presence. This means we come alongside them, support them, and hold them up.

In our gardens, we can drive a stake in the ground next to a weak plant and tie them together for support. We can also do this in prayer, holding them up to the Father when we get in His presence. However, we can carry them no further than the cross. Only Jesus can take their burdens away. We cannot do that part. If you try to carry someone else's burden, you are not casting it on Jesus. He is the only one who saves. He put His stake in the ground, stretched out His hands, and said, "I'll carry it, and I'll cast it as far as the east is from the west" (Psalm 103:12 GNT).

And pray in the Spirit on all occasions with all kinds of prayers and requests. With this in mind, be alert and always keep on praying for all the Lord's people (Ephesians 6:18).

Another type of intercession, called spiritual warfare, deals with the evil forces in the heavenly realm (Ephesians 6:12). This type is not about carrying burdens but about closing doors to evil and coming against those forces. We do this through both prayer and worship.

Let's look at prayer first. When we enter into spiritual warfare, we must remember two important things. First, we must put on the full armor of God so we can stand firm (Ephesians 6:10-17). Next, we must know where our position is. "For He raised us from the dead along with Christ and seated us with him in the heavenly realms because we are united with Christ Jesus" (Ephesians 2:6). Wearing God's own armor, seated in heavenly places, we are equipped to close those doors and ready to go to battle against the enemy on behalf of our family, friends, and whoever else God brings to our minds.

Can you now see why it's important to know who you are in Christ, the authority you have, and the power available to you through the Holy Spirit? These low-lying demons and spirits are nothing for a warrior of God to be afraid of. But if you don't know who you are, they can be frightening. You need to know that God has not given us a spirit of fear but of power and love and of a sound mind (2 Timothy 1:7 NKJV). To be effective in this battle, you won't use your hands. You'll use your mouth, activated by faith.

The Bible says to humble yourselves before God. Resist the devil, and he will flee from you (James 4:7). A position of authority requires humility before God. Do you bow to His authority first and foremost? You resist the devil by turning from sin. This also closes a door to the activity of evil spirits in your own life. When the door is closed in your life, you can help others.

Let the redeemed of the Lord say so whom He has redeemed from the hand of the enemy (Psalm 107:2).

When God has delivered you from the enemy, not only can you tell others about what He's done, but you can stand in your position and authority as one who has been redeemed to help others get their deliverance. Only from a place of humility and living for God can you become this warrior and come against evil.

Now that you're in position, wield the Sword of the Spirit (God's Word) to strike a cutting blow to evil spirits. Know who you are and declare through your words where your victory comes from.

If God is for us, who can be against us? He who did not spare his own Son, but gave him up for us all—how will he not also, along with him, graciously give us all things? Who will bring any charge against those whom God has chosen? It is God who justifies. Who then is the one who condemns? No one. Christ Jesus who died—more than that, who was raised to life—is at the right hand of God and is also interceding for us. Who shall separate us from the love of Christ? Shall trouble or hardship or persecution or famine or nakedness or danger or sword?. . . No, in all these things we are more than conquerors through him who loved us (Romans 8:31-37).

In addition to God's Word, worship is also a weapon. Worshipping and praising God makes the enemy flee. Let's look at two places in the Bible where a battle was won through worship. The first is the battle at Jericho. You can read this account in Joshua 6. The Lord instructed Joshua to have all the people march around the city for seven days. They were to put the Ark of the covenant at the front of the line. Priest with horns went before and after the Ark. For six days, they marched in silence, but on the seventh day, they blew their horns and lifted a shout to the Lord. The walls of Jericho fell "For the Lord has given you the town!" (Joshua 6:16). Notice, when you put God first and give Him a shout of praise, the walls of the enemy are destroyed. There is nothing he can erect that can stand up to your shouts of praise.

Another battle can be found in 2 Chronicles 20. In this battle the king appointed singers to walk ahead of the army, singing to the Lord and praising Him. Now there is a battle plan you probably won't see in our military's play book, but if they only knew. It says in verse 22 that "At the very moment they began to sing and give praise, the Lord caused the armies of Ammon, Moab, and Mount Seir to start fighting among themselves." Praise and worship confuses the enemy; in fact, your enemies will begin to attack each other. When the enemy knows that the Lord Himself fights against him on your behalf, look what the Bible says.

When all the surrounding kingdoms heard that the Lord himself had fought against the enemies of Israel, the fear of God came over them. So Jehoshaphat's kingdom was at peace, for his God had given him rest on every side (2 Chronicles 20:29-30).

Friends, it is possible to have peace on every side during your battle if you use worship as a weapon. It takes great humility to worship when everything in you says fight. We always think if we're not fighting then we're not doing anything to help our situation. Next time consider praising, thanking, and worshiping and watch God go to battle on your behalf and enjoy the peace He brings as the enemy flees. In fact, he doesn't just flee; he has to scatter!

The Lord will cause your enemies who rise against you to be defeated before your face; they shall come out against you one way and flee before you seven ways (Deuteronomy 28:7).

He cannot remain in the presence of worship. Play worship music in your home and anywhere you want to drive out evil spirits. Praise confounds the enemy and strikes another powerful blow. When you worship instead of worrying, he is confused. When you praise instead of blaming, he is dumbfounded. He doesn't understand when you speak out of love and not anger. He knows nothing about love. When you refuse to act in his ways, choosing God's ways instead, it's as if you become invisible to the enemy. He can no longer see you because when you begin worshipping and God's presence fills the atmosphere, you have just entered the secret place. The enemy can't find you when you're in the secret place because you are hidden in Christ.

Why is it important to be hidden? Because someone is looking for you. When you start your day in the secret place, your day is productive and protected. If you don't start your day in that place, you become visible to the enemy and subject to his schemes. You come out of hiding and he says, "Ah-ha! There you are. I see you." You want to remain hidden and protected in battle. Psalm 91 holds wonderful promises for those who dwell in the secret place:

Those who live in the shelter of the Most High will find rest in the shadow of the Almighty. This I declare about the Lord: He alone is my refuge, my place of safety; he is my God, and I trust him. For he will rescue you from every trap and protect you from deadly disease. He will cover you with his feathers. He will shelter you with his wings. His faithful promises are your armor and protection (Psalm 91:1-4 NLT).

Not only does God shelter and protect you, but His word also says, "You prepare a feast for me in the presence of my enemies" (Psalm 23:5). This means God displays His love for you like a banquet and makes the enemy watch Him bless you. The enemy is jealous of you. He wanted to be like God, but God created you to be like Him. The enemy hates you because of it. Worship is a lavish display of your love for God and His love for you, and this strikes a blow to the enemy. Worshipping says nothing can separate you from the love of God. The enemy is no match for the son or daughter hidden in Christ, confident in their identity and authority, who possesses an arsenal of God's Word and praises for Him.

The Censer

In Layer Three, we are golden censers. In the Old Testament tabernacle, the closer you got to the Holy of Holies, the purer the materials. Priests entered the Most Holy Place with censers made of pure gold. As we get closer to God in His presence, He purifies us, making us holy as He is holy (1 Peter 1:16). The priest entered the Holy of Holies once a year to make atonement for the entire nation of Israel. He interceded for them because they could not go in and do it for themselves. In this layer, we're interceding for others. To do that, our hearts and motives must be pure.

How should our prayers look in this layer? In Layer One, we began by casting all our cares. This time we bring someone else's cares with us and lay them down. Our God is big enough to take the things we sacrifice as well as those things sacrificed for others. For example, you may be concerned about your marriage. Pray something like,

> Lord, I give You my marriage. I lay down my will and the way things should look, and I make this sacrifice not only for me, but also for my spouse. Bring us both into the unity You desire for us and for all marriages. I lift up the marriages of my friends and family members, that they too would have unified marriages ac-

cording to Your will.

At this point, it's good to turn on some worship music and go deeper into His presence. Ask God to bring to mind any people in your life who need prayer. You might already have a prayer list but also be open to praying for anyone God wants you to pray for. When you feel the Spirit's prompting, begin from your authority and position. Remind God for whom you are praying and present their need, as if before a judge.

Here's an example of intercession:

Lord, I am Your beloved child and representative on this earth. I lift up my mother, who is in the hospital. I present her to You as Your child, saved by grace, and I intercede on her behalf for healing. Jesus, You are the Great Physician, and I ask You now to cover her with Your healing blood—the blood You shed on the cross that made us whole. I enforce that victory now on my mom's behalf. Your words are life to those who find them and health to one's whole body. I speak Your words of life now. Let healing come, in the name of Jesus.

If you are engaging in spiritual warfare, it might look something like this:

Lord, You have given me authority to trample on snakes and crush the head of the serpent. Every evil spirit is under my feet in the name of Jesus. I come against the spirit of chaos, which has come against my son, and I uproot it in the name of Jesus. Your Word

says that anything You have not planted must be up-
rooted. I declare that he has the mind of Christ, for
You have given him the spirit of a sound mind. I declare single focus to come into his mind. No more
double focus. I plead the blood of Jesus over his mind.
Every spirit that is not of God must leave now, in the
name of Jesus, and go where He tells him.

After you have prayed for everyone, end by thanking God
for what He has done and for hearing and working on your
behalf. You must always ask Him to fill the people you have
prayed for with the Holy Spirit and ask for their protection
and yours. Praise Him for His goodness, faithfulness, mercy,
and anything else pertaining to your situation. Sit and rest in
His presence. Wait to see if He wants to reveal anything to
you about the things you've prayed. When you feel a release
in your spirit, say, "Amen."

∽ Twelve ∽

WALL: WATCHERS ON THE WALL AND GOD IS MY WALL OF FIRE

I looked for a man among them who would build up the wall and stand before me in the gap on behalf of the land so I would not have to destroy it, but I found none (Ezekiel 22:30).

The wall is our protection. It surrounds us personally, but it can also surround an entire church, community, region, state, or nation. That's why it's important to have intercessors standing guard on the wall. The wall of our neighbor, community, or nation may not be complete to provide that protection. It may have gaps or broken areas, so the intercessor will come and stand in the gap.

In Layer Three, we are called to be intercessors or "watchers on the wall." If God compels you to pray for others or puts a passion in your heart for the needs of your community or nation, then He has just posted you on the wall to fill the gaps where the enemy can come in. The wall is no longer weak because someone who is strong in prayer has just filled that gap. As you stand in the gap for others, know that someone is standing in the gap for you. Where your wall is broken, God has assigned an intercessor to fill the gap. You may already know who that is, and you may also already know the one for whom God has appointed you to intercede.

In the Bible, the watchers are trained to spot two things: messengers (2 Samuel 18:24-26) and the approach of the enemy (Nehemiah 4). Watchmen need discernment so they'll know if a message or word is from God or from the enemy (1 John 4:1). The enemy can come in many forms, including an evil spirit, a false prophet (Matthew 7:15), or a false teacher. Discernment can help you identify who you're dealing with and weed out the little subtleties of the lies. We cannot have this discernment without the help of the Holy Spirit. Discernment will help us not to be led astray, as the Bible warns.

> *Keep watch over yourselves and all the flock of which the Holy Spirit has made you overseers. Be shepherds of the church of God, which he bought with his own blood. . . Even from your own number men will arise and distort the truth in order to draw away disciples after them* (Acts 20:28, 30).

> *Therefore, dear friends, since you have been forewarned, be on your guard so that you may not be carried away by the error of the lawless and fall from your secure position. But grow in the grace and knowledge of our Lord and Savior Jesus Christ* (2 Peter 3:17-18).

I had a friend who started listening to a certain preacher on the internet. As he explained some of the revelatory messages he'd heard, many alarms went off in my head. I felt a check inside my spirit every time I heard something that was "sort of right" but not exactly right. It is not hard to discern right from wrong, but discerning right from almost right is a lot harder.

My friend began to listen to this preacher exclusively. A teacher should always point you to Jesus, not to himself. A teacher should lead you toward dependence on God, not dependence on his teaching. The enemy as a false teacher is dangerous because he doesn't come dressed like a wolf. You don't know you're in danger, because he comes in sheep's clothing (Matthew 7:15). He looks and sounds just like you. The Bible also says he can come as an angel of light. Satan himself masquerades as an angel of light (2 Corinthians 11:14).

Have you ever had an opportunity that seemed too good to be true? I have. Surely, this must be from God, right?

Every time one of these opportunities presented itself, I got lured away from what I was previously doing—from the place where God had put me. Each time, it ended in failure and disappointment. You can't always discern this for yourself. You need a watchman on your wall.

However, the enemy may not come as a false messenger or an angel of light. He might come at you with an outright attack. A watchman will help discern if someone is under a spiritual attack or if their situation is due to sin or uncontrollable circumstances. We often diagnose our problem inaccurately and need help and spiritual guidance in order to ascertain the truth.

Closing doors to evil in our homes and lives is the first step in fighting evil. When we live closely with God, repent from sin, and purify our lives as suggested in Layers One and Two, available open doors to the enemy are limited. The enemy's bait is usually offense. When other people offend us, the enemy slams the trap door. Then we spiral into resentment, bitterness, and hatred, which lead to unforgiveness. We must be on guard against offenses because the minute we are offended, the enemy knows he has won.

For years, a growing resentment toward my sister-in-law kept me from experiencing the peace, freedom, and destiny God meant me to have. It started from a place of jealousy and offense. Everything she did offended me because of my jealousy toward her. I watched as she got all the things I wanted out of life, and I had to wait. I judged her out of my offense. I never gave her the benefit of the doubt, even though I extended much grace toward others.

The root of bitterness grew until the day God began to work on my heart. I felt it was time to forgive her, and as my heart softened to this, God also showed me I needed to ask her forgiveness. Well, I did not want to do that! However, if we have even a little offense, jealousy, resentment, or bitterness, God cannot use us.

In time, I did ask for her forgiveness. Today, we are the best of friends. A day doesn't go by when we don't have an hour-long conversation. God is our common denominator, and He is using us both in mighty ways to pray and intercede for others.

Do you think the enemy knew God's plans for us? You bet he did! That's why he set his trap, and I took the bait. If you need to reconcile with someone, do it today. Life on the other side is so much better. Your stolen destiny waits for you.

Can you see why we cannot give the enemy room to place

his bait? When we close doors to sin and offense in our lives, we can help others close those doors as well. One effective way to help is to anoint their home and property, asking for the forgiveness of sins and requesting assignments of angels for their protection. We may even have to repent on their behalf. Our intercession can help others become right with the Lord. This is exactly what Aaron did when God sent a plague against the people in the wilderness because of their rebellion.

And Moses said to Aaron, "Quick, take an incense burner (censor) and place burning coals on it from the altar. Lay incense on it, and carry it out among the people to purify them and make them right with the Lord... The plague had already begun to strike down the people, but Aaron burned the incense and purified the people (Numbers 16:46-47).

You can read about the whole account in Numbers 16. Only Aaron could do this because of his authority as a priest. Friends, we are a royal priesthood, so we have this authority in intercession.

We may need to engage in spiritual warfare to break the enemy's hold and thwart his plans against that person. By binding the enemy in the name of Jesus, we make his efforts ineffective and render him impotent.

Then we loose God's plan over the person's life, replacing the enemy's activity with God's activity. As God's partner in prayer, we have the authority to bind and loose, aligning the reality of earth and heaven, letting "His kingdom come; His will be done on earth as it is in heaven" (Matthew 6:10).

And I will give you the keys (authority) of the Kingdom of Heaven. Whatever you bind (forbid) on earth will be bound (forbidden) in heaven, and whatever you loose (permit) on earth will be loosed (permitted) in heaven (Matthew 16:19).

If something is not allowed in heaven, like sickness, poverty, and fear, then it is not allowed on earth. But it takes someone with the authority of heaven to enforce it. You have that kind of authority when you operate as God's partner. As you honor Him, He honors you, and He will not put you to shame (Isaiah 54:4).

Our prayers activate His work, and His work validates our prayers. Could He be waiting for us to understand this kind of partnership so His will can be done on earth as it is in heaven? As I pondered this question, a new confidence arose. I considered stepping out to pray for others, and I realized that "me and Jesus got this!" It's me and Him—Him and me. I need Him to do what only He can do, but He needs me to do my part too. I've got to pray. I've got to decree and declare. I've got to bind and loose. I have to enforce His victory through my authority. For whatever reason, from the beginning of creation, God chose man to partner with Him for all He intends to do on the earth. If you were the enemy, wouldn't you do everything you could to keep us from knowing our position? As we rise up, God arises and scatters the enemy through us. You don't need to fear the enemy. He is afraid of you.

"And I myself will be a wall of fire around it," declares the Lord, "and I will be its glory within" (Zechariah 2:5).

As we engage in spiritual warfare, God becomes our wall of fire, and we can ask for His protection against retaliation from the enemy. As you come against him, he will mount a counterattack. But then God surrounds us like a hedge—a burning hedge of protection. For the Lord is faithful; He will strengthen you and guard you from the evil one (2 Thessalonians 3:3)—not only guard us but fight for us (Nehemiah 4:20). We can hold onto this promise found in the book of Isaiah.

But in that coming day no weapon turned against you will succeed. You will silence every voice raised up to accuse you. These benefits are enjoyed by the servants of the Lord; their vindication will come from me. I, the Lord, have spoken! (Isaiah 54:17)

I believe every promise in the Bible. But when it is followed by, "I, the Lord, have spoken," there is no questioning that promise. You can place your confidence in the Lord to have your back when you are in battle. In fact, have you noticed that the armor of God doesn't cover your backside? You don't need anything there, because God Himself has your back.

Thoughts on Layer Three

We've come a long way from not knowing who we are to walking in our authority and releasing His power. We've gone from protecting ourselves with the lies of our strongholds, built out of pain and hurt, to having God protect us with His fire. God has formed our vessel and given us something to carry. In Layer Three, we pour it out on others. He provides the anointing we're to walk in and the grace (operational power) as we pour into others. He gives us armor so we can take our stand against the enemy and his schemes, and He stands right behind us as our rear guard when we do (Isaiah 52:12). He never forsakes us, never lets us down, and never puts us to shame. When we take the focus off ourselves, God awakens us to what He wants to do on this earth, leads us as His Spirit rests upon us, and provides us with His authority, power, and protection. How amazing to go this deep with God.

Would you believe me if I told you there's still more? When I asked God to take me deeper, I wasn't sure what that would look like. But as I ventured in, He revealed that going deeper meant a deeper level of intimacy. It all happens in the secret place. You must be vulnerable enough to bare all in His presence—completely vulnerable, completely surrendered, and completely open to this level of intimacy.

In the parable of the ten virgins found in Matthew 25:1-13, five of the ten virgins had to buy more oil. They did not bring enough to meet the Bridegroom. Because of the delay of His coming, they ran out. The oil represents intimacy. We cannot rely on others to give it to us; we have to have enough intimacy with Jesus ourselves. We do not know the hour of His second coming, so what do we do while we wait? We engage in intimacy in the secret place, so when He comes for us, He will recognize us. Do not tire or fall asleep. Do not run out of oil. The last thing we want is for Jesus to say, "I never knew you." Jesus is coming back for His bride. If you want to be found with plenty of oil, then let's go deeper.

Discussion Questions:

1. What differences have you noticed when you pray God's promises and speak God's Word over your situations?

2. How can you determine where God is working? Do you see areas where He is working in your church or community? How can you join Him? What has He put on your heart to do?

3. What has been your previous understanding about authority? How do you now understand it? What do you believe is your authority? How do you feel about the Great Commission? What was your understanding of it before, and what is your understanding of it now?

4. What do you need to do differently in worship to get a breakthrough or go deeper into God's presence?

5. What do you think is important to be aware of when engaging in spiritual warfare? How is fighting the enemy different than fighting in the world?

6. How can you be confident that God will show up when you pray for someone? What part does authority play in it? What part does obedience play? What part does belief play?

7. How are the duties of the watchman helpful for intercessors? How might the enemy try to come against you? How does God protect you?

8. What do you identify with most in this layer? What do you still struggle to understand?

Layer Four

CARRYING HIS GLORY AND OPERATING UNDER AN OPEN HEAVEN

∼ *Thirteen* ∼

TEMPLE: RIVERS OF LIVING WATER

If anyone is thirsty, let him come to me and drink. Whoever believes in me, as the scriptures has said, streams of living water will flow from within him." By this he meant the Spirit, whom those who believed in him were later to receive (John 7:38-39).

Jesus has living water. The living water is the Holy Spirit. When Jesus gives it to us through the baptism, He comes and rests on us. We sense His promptings, and He anoints us for the benefit of others.

But there is yet another dimension of the Holy Spirit. That dimension is in the rivers. When we operate in the fullness of the Holy Spirit, rivers of living water flow from within us. We become a conduit for His Spirit—a type of extension cord that, once plugged in, allows His power to flow freely.

You shall receive power when the Holy Spirit has come upon you (Acts 1:8 NKJV).

Smith Wigglesworth said it like this in his devotional:

> The baptism in the Holy Spirit is to possess us so that we are, and may be continually, so full of the Holy Spirit that utterances and revelations and eyesight and everything else may be so remarkably controlled by the Spirit of God that we live and move in this glorious sphere of usefulness for the glory of God.

Being in the rivers is where we live and move and have our being (Acts 17:28). The glory of God flows within the rivers, and the baptism releases us into that flow. Just as He transforms from glory to glory through the depths of the layers (His presence), He also moves us from faith to anointing to glory. Our faith ushers in His anointing, and the practice of our anointing brings us into the glory. Because of the baptism of the Holy Spirit, we can now live up to our full potential in Christ.

In Layer Three, we discussed the importance of tuning in to our natural senses to "feel" the Holy Spirit. We must be in tune with our spiritual senses as well, having spiritual eyes to see and spiritual ears to hear. God speaks to us in many ways, including His Word, circumstances, and the words of others. But when our spiritual senses are trained, He shows us other ways He wants to speak. One way is through nature. You might think that is a natural way, but if our spirits are in tune with God, we can sense Him in nature.

One day, while I was in my backyard, I noticed three dragonflies. This was interesting because I don't have a lake or other water source in my yard. Immediately, I sensed the Lord was trying to tell me something because there were three dragonflies, and the number three is significant to the Lord. It represents divine wholeness, completeness, and perfection, like the Trinity. It also represents putting a divine stamp of completion or fulfillment on a subject. I was in the middle of writing this book, and I knew what He was telling me. Then a few days later, I saw about thirty dragonflies (give or take as I did not count them) flying in my backyard. Instantly, I knew God wanted to say something about the dragonflies.

I did some research and discovered the dragonfly has a scurrying flight across the water as if looking beyond what's on the surface into what lies deeper. Dragonflies also absorb warmth from the sun and reflect it through their wings. This is a symbol of growth and development. When we stay close to our Source, we reflect His light to guide others. The dragonfly perfectly represents the purpose of this book, and by showing me a multitude of the original three, the Lord revealed that many people will grow and develop as the dragonflies and will begin to do the same. That's a prophetic word of declaration for you. Receive it! I never would have received that message from God if my spiritual senses hadn't been tuned in to God as He speaks through nature. I could have just thought the dragonflies were nice, or worse yet, not noticed them at all.

He also wants us to see with spiritual eyes and hear with spiritual ears. We need to perceive the invisible and the silent. Instead of seeing the circumstances around us, we need to see God working in those circumstances. Shifting our focus and our gaze will activate our spiritual eyes.

We see a great example of this in 2 Kings chapter six. The king of Aram sent his troops against Elisha because the prophet kept foiling the king's plans to attack Israel, revealing them prophetically to the king of Israel. When the army approached, Elisha's servant was afraid of the army on the ground. Take a look at verse 16 to see what happened:

"Don't be afraid!" Elisha told him. "For there are more on our side than on theirs!" Then Elisha prayed, "O Lord, open his eyes and let him see!" The Lord opened the young man's eyes, and when he looked up, he saw that the hillside around Elisha was filled with horses and chariots of fire (1 Kings 6:16 NLT).

The enemy works low, on the ground, and in the world. We cannot continue to look there and expect to flow in the rivers. When we "look up" to God, He begins to show us activity in the heavenly realm. Because we are seated in the heavenly realm, we have a great vantage point, but we must look from that vantage point (Colossians 3:1-2).

The enemy would have us focus on our condition instead of our position. The truth is, by focusing on our position in Christ, we will have the power to change our condition. Abraham did not look to his or Sarah's condition when God told him he would be a father of many nations. They were elderly, and their condition revealed they were far too old to have children. Instead, he lifted his gaze to the heavens where the promise of God said, "I will make your descendants as numerous as the starts in the sky, and I will give them all these lands, and through your offspring all nations on earth will be blessed" (Genesis 26:4). By adjusting their focus onto God and His promise, Abraham and Sarah conceived Isaac, creating a new condition, one that fulfilled the promise.

Tuning out the negative, defeating voice of the enemy and listening to God's perspective will activate our spiritual ears. Wisdom is different than knowledge. People hear in the natural to learn and gain knowledge, but God gives wisdom. The only way we can hear wisdom is to develop our spiritual ears and receive God's truth. "Incline your ear and come to Me. Listen, that you may live" (Isaiah 55:3 NASB).

God's wisdom produces life. Death can come if we rely only on worldly knowledge, logical persuasion, and our own understanding. The Bible states, "As the heavens are higher than the earth, so are my ways higher than your ways and my thoughts higher than your thoughts" (Isaiah 55:9). Trust in the Lord with all your heart and do not depend on your own understanding (Proverbs 3:5 NLT).

We need to raise our thoughts higher and listen with spiritual ears. If we are to flow in the rivers, we cannot use our own words to counsel or comfort others. They are not looking for us but for Christ within us. Spiritual eyes and ears help us to see higher and hear clearly.

We need to open our spiritual senses. Jesus was so aware of the Holy Spirit upon Him that the Spirit never left Him. In fact, He was so aware that he could feel power releasing from Him, as He did with the woman who had the issue of blood (Mark 5:24-30). How wonderful to be in a place where the Holy Spirit never leaves us but continually flows. That's what God wants for us, and it is possible. Acts 5:15-16 tells us that when Peter walked down the street, people were healed when his shadow fell upon them. Did his shadow heal them? No; rather, the Holy Spirit rested upon Peter and flowed through him.

When we feel the Holy Spirit upon us, or we get the

"unction," as Smith Wigglesworth said, that is our invitation to join the Holy Spirit in what He wants to do in that moment. I'll never forget the first time I felt the unction. A friend was telling me of some unusual experiences and feelings she'd been having. This was clearly the enemy trying to oppress her. All of a sudden, an unfamiliar feeling struck me—what I now call a quickening in my spirit. Feeling antsy, excited, and nervous, I couldn't sit still in my seat. I just blurted out, "I have to pray for you right now!"

As I prayed, God ministered to her and healed her, breaking off a few things as well. I could see and sense it all. God wants to possess us with this flowing river so we're ready to release His power at a moment's notice. When the unction comes, our response is to obey and let God do His part. We are responsible for only our part, not His.

During this time, the unction was strong, and I couldn't help but obey. But it will not always be that strong. It can also be so subtle that, if your senses are not tuned in, you could miss it. You will not want to miss a move of God. I once missed out on a huge move of God, and I've been kicking myself ever since. I often wonder what would have happened if I had followed through with what He asked me to do.

When I first felt this prompting, I thought it was outrageous. I was traveling home for my high school friend's funeral. On the drive, while worshipping God, I heard in my spirit that He wanted me to raise my friend from the dead. Let me tell you, the unction held a lot more nervousness than excitement. Had God just asked me to raise my friend from the dead?

The unction did not go away, not even in my disbelief. God does not mind disbelief or questioning. What you absolutely cannot have is unbelief. So I said, "Lord, if you want me to do this, you'll have to strengthen me in my spirit. Increase my capacity to believe!"

Well, do you know what He did? The next worship song that came on YouTube was "This is a Move" by Tasha Combs. This is the first time I had ever heard that song. I heard her sing "Bodies are still being raised." What? She went on to sing that about five more times, but to me, it seemed like a hundred.

I said, "God, if you want me to do this, You'll have to give me someone to pray for first, and then You'll have to show up so I know you're with me."

God is always with us. In fact, He's there ahead of us, waiting for us. You learn lessons like this when you give God an ultimatum.

I was meeting a group of high school friends that night for dinner, since we see each other only once every ten years at our reunion. Then the mood turned serious as one our friends told us he had cancer. Quickening! Unction! Nervousness! Antsy excitement!

"I have to pray for you right now," I said.

The others wanted to join in as well. None of us had any idea what was about to happen. Rivers flowed through me as I prayed with authority, and the Holy Spirit fell on two of my friends with weeping.

I stayed up and prayed most of the night, unable to believe what God was going to do. I didn't even know how to pray for anything like that. The next day, when I walked into that funeral, I was never so relieved to see that someone had been cremated. I wondered if God was just testing me to see if I would do it. I never attempted to pray. Later I wondered if I had missed it.

I believe that in this example, I was thinking I was going to have to operate under a special anointing. Understand that God wants to display Himself through you and promises to be with you.

Don't be afraid, for I am with you. Don't be discouraged, for I am your God. I will strengthen you and help you. I will hold you up with my victorious right hand (Isaiah 41:10 NLT).

I thought He intended for me to do it. If God says, "I'll be with you," it's because He's giving you an impossible task only He can do. I never knew if God healed my friend from cancer, but I saw one of those friends a year later, and she had stopped drinking and lost forty pounds. Sometimes you never know what the Holy Spirit wants to do. There is a time for laboring and working, but there also is a time of resting and ease as we go where the Spirit carries us. It's the difference between swimming and surfing.

Joshua Mills says it this way in his book *Moving in Glory Realms*: "The anointing enables us to swim in the river of God. We swim in that river, doing the best we can, empowered by the Holy Spirit's anointing. When the glory arrives, it actually disables us, because when it comes, we surf on the waves of the Spirit's flow." What a beautiful picture of another level of partnership with the Holy Spirit.

You might be asking yourself, "What is this anointing? How do I know if I have it?" These are the spiritual gifts. You might have natural talents, and the Holy Spirit will put an anointing on those talents, enhancing them. When that happens, they are considered spiritual gifts.

111

All the gifts are for service to others. Spiritual gifts are portions of God's grace (operational power). You may have one or two gifts, supernaturally enhanced beyond your natural talent. Things that you could not do before, or at least not as well as you can now. This is your anointing. God chose it for you so He could express His operational power (grace) through you. People can be talented or gifted musicians or they can be anointed musicians. People can be talented or gifted speakers or they can be anointed speakers. God's glory flows and manifests through anointing, not talent. In essence, God ignites a fire in the person, then they use their talents or gifts as "sent ones" to glorify God and help people. When we carry His presence and fire through His anointing, we can surf on His glory.

The Holy Spirit gives gifts as He chooses. But the Bible instructs us to desire all the gifts earnestly and eagerly (1 Corinthians 14:1). If you want a particular gift, you can ask Him for it. The key is to value the gifts He's already given us. When we use those gifts for the benefit of others and we value them, we can ask for more. When the Lord sees that He can trust us with a little, He knows He can trust us with much (Luke 16:10). We should always desire more. The more we receive, the closer we get to operating in the fullness of the Holy Spirit as Jesus did.

> *And the Spirit of the Lord will rest on him—the Spirit of wisdom and understanding, the Spirit of counsel and might, the Spirit of knowledge and fear of the Lord* (Isaiah 11:2).

These seven spirits are the characteristics of God that

represent His fullness displayed in the person of the Holy Spirit resting upon Jesus. We can have the fullness resting upon us too. Notice the Holy Spirit was always with Jesus, and He will always be with us as we walk in this fullness.

The seven Spirits seem to also represent the rivers of living water. If the living water is the Holy Spirit, then the rivers (notice plural) of living waters must be these seven characteristics each representing one river. Together, they represent the fullness of one Holy Spirit. The number seven has great significance in the Bible. It represents perfection, totality, or completion. The seven Spirits speak of the perfection of the Holy Spirit. So when rivers of living water flow through us, we see a river of the Lord, a river of wisdom, a river of understanding, a river of counsel, a river of might, a river of knowledge, and a river of fear (awe and reverence) of the Lord. These are the things we need when ministering to others. Keep asking for more until you see these rivers flow through you.

≈ *Fourteen* ≈

WORSHIP: WORSHIP IN SPIRIT AND TRUTH AND THE HOLY SPIRIT DIRECTS MY PRAYERS

Yet a time is coming and has now come when the true worshippers will worship the Father in spirit and truth, for they are true worshippers the Father seeks. God is spirit, and his worshipper must worship in spirit and truth (John 4:23-24).

In the Old Testament, the place of worship was important. First the Israelites focused on the tabernacle, the temple, or a mountain. Then they fought over which mountain or which city to worship in. They didn't get it.

Today, people fight over music styles or which church is better. They don't get it either. It's not about where you worship. You don't need a place to go in order to worship God. He wants you to worship Him while in His presence. When you receive the indwelling of the Holy Spirit, your spirit will immediately want to praise God. The worship will come from your spirit, not an outside source. You are not looking for a directive on how to worship. You just worship out of an overflow of the well (presence of God). When you sing with your whole being, His joy floods through. "In His presence is fullness of joy; at His right hand are pleasures evermore" (Psalm 16:11 NASB). You cannot hold onto the contents of a cup that is overflowing. This type of worship cannot be contained. The Father is looking for those who will worship in that way (John 4:23).

God first invites us to enter into His presence, and then He invites us to come up higher. When we do this, we can know and pray the heart of the Father.

Moses is a great example of one who accepted the invitation to come up higher (Exodus 19). God invited him up on a mountaintop where He gave him the Ten Commandments. God revealed His laws to the one who dared to come up higher. He wanted to be with all the people and speak with them, but the people were afraid. They wanted Moses to go up and then tell them what He said.

How about you? Are you satisfied with someone else's encounter with God, with someone else's revelation? I know I'm not! I want revelation for myself. I want amazing God encounters. Moses received His promises and saw His power while in His presence, but he wasn't satisfied until he saw His glory (Exodus 33:18).

Moses wanted the Person. We have to move away from wanting just what God can do for us and instead, begin to want God. Moses hungered for the intimate knowledge of God. To know Him in this way is not to study about Him but to experience Him. In fact, Jesus defines this as eternal life.

> *Now this is eternal life: that they know you, the only true God, and Jesus Christ, whom you have sent* (John 17:3).

If we know God intimately, we experience eternal life now. It all starts with entering in, then coming up higher in the Spirit. I don't know about you, but while in His presence, I want to get a glimpse of heaven. I want to enter the throne room of God. We can do that! The Spirit will take us there.

> *After these things I looked, and behold, a door standing open in heaven, and the first voice which I had heard, like the sound of a trumpet speaking with me, said, "come up here, and I will show you what must take place after these things." Immediately I was in the Spirit; and behold, a throne was standing in heaven, and One sitting on the throne* (Revelation 4:1-2).

I want to see His glory. When Moses came down the mountain, his face glowed from being so close to God's glory (Exodus 34:29). You cannot be that close to God and not be changed. Jesus' disciples were also changed when He, Peter, James, and John went up the mountain to be with God (Matthew 17:1-2). When they went "up higher," they saw Jesus transfigured in His glory. They heard the voice of God and received revelation about Jesus's true identity. The Lord makes this available to those who will go higher. Jesus will be revealed.

God will reveal His plans, blueprints, and strategies, as well as His heart, in this higher place. Surely the sovereign Lord does nothing without revealing His plan to His servants the prophets (Amos 3:7). Daniel received interpretations of dreams (Daniel 2), visions (Daniel 8), and strategies for prayer to bring the Israelites out of captivity (Daniel 9). God wants to communicate with us through dreams as well.

I will pour out my Spirit upon all people. Your sons and daughters will prophesy. Your old men will dream dreams, and your young men will see visions. In those days I will pour out my Spirit even on servants—men and women alike (Joel 2:28-29).

A few months ago, God began to communicate with me in a new way through dreams. Before this, I never remembered my dreams. Maybe you don't remember yours either. Do you know why? It could be a combination of things. Ask God to send His angels as messengers in the night to give you dreams. Psalm 104:4 calls His messengers winds, and in another version, He calls angels winds. So, we can determine that these winds are angels, and these angels are His messengers. Ask for them!

Second, as soon as you wake up, try to remember your dream, even just a small detail. This might help you remember more of the dream. Do this before you get out of bed. Once you start your day, it becomes harder to remember. The enemy would love nothing more than to steal your dreams because they are messages from God. Satan will do all he can to steal them from you and prevent you from receiving the message.

If the enemy has stolen your dreams, you have a right to get them back. You can start dreaming again. When I asked God to help me remember my dreams, they came back like a flood. I have one almost every night.

Next, ask for the interpretation. The dreams may seem like nonsense. Or you might mistakenly think you know what the dream means. Be sure to pray and see what God reveals. My dreams started as dreams for myself, like Joseph's in Genesis 37. Eventually, He gave me dreams for others. I couldn't understand them because they weren't about me. Then eventually, God revealed who they were for. When God gives you dreams, you can speak life into other people. Ask Him to give you the ability to interpret other people's dreams as He did for Joseph and Daniel. Dreams are another way God can reveal His heart to the one who will come up higher.

We are to share some revelations but not all. Always ask God to show you whether you should share them. Sometimes God gives revelation so you can prevail in prayer. When you let the Spirit direct your prayers, you know what's on His heart, and then you can pray. He directs your prayers for the purpose of prevailing. Prevailing is not a one-time short prayer. Prevailing is persistence in prayer until you get the answer or the thing is done. You will feel compelled to pray, and the Spirit will let you know when it's time to stop.

Praying in the Spirit is useful in all types of prayer, but it's essential when we prevail in prayer for God's heart. We receive the gift of tongues upon our baptism in the Holy Spirit. We all need to operate in this gift. This is your secret prayer language between God and you. The enemy cannot understand what you're saying when you pray in the Spirit. It gives you and God privacy that you do not have when you pray in your natural language.

Sometimes we don't know what to pray or how to pray effectively, so the Holy Spirit directs our prayer language, interpreting and translating our prayers in a way that lines up with God's will. When God shows us something that's on His heart, we may not understand it because it didn't generate from our heart. This is the perfect time to pray in the Spirit and let the Holy Spirit direct our praying.

The Holy Spirit helps us in our weakness. For example, we don't know what God wants us to pray for. But the Holy Spirit prays for us with groaning that can't be expressed in words. And the Father who knows all hearts knows what the Spirit is saying, for the Spirit pleads for us believers in harmony with God's own will (Romans 8:26-27 NLT).

If you don't think you have a prayer language, don't panic. You do; it just hasn't manifested yet. The Bible says speaking in tongues is a sign of being baptized with the Holy Spirit. In fact, it can be the initial sign (Acts 2:4, Acts 19:2-6), but not always. It is important to understand that this is the gift the Spirit gives, but it may not manifest itself immediately. You may have received it but are not operating in it yet.

When I received the baptism of the Holy Spirit, tongues did not manifest immediately. They came almost a year later through prayer. I had to pray for them to come into operation because, although I didn't know it, something was blocking it.

"Manifesting" refers to the outward expression of God. He can manifest through His gifts, His presence, and His glory. Manifestations are nothing to fear or mock. It's how God chooses to express Himself outwardly. If you don't expect this gift, it can be scary or confusing when your tongue starts to move and your mind is not directing it. This is just the Spirit releasing His gift of tongues to you.

I expected it, but thought I hadn't received. Then God revealed the block. I am careful with my words, and I value the eloquent speech and articulation God gave me. I was afraid of not being in control of my words and of looking foolish. When I realized this, I decided I wanted to value the spiritual gift more, so I surrendered my tongue to Him and asked Him to take over.

I began to say over and over, "Thank You, Jesus!" The block was released, and strange sounds came tumbling out of my mouth. I tried to go back to saying "Thank You." But my tongue would not form those words, so I continued letting the strange language flow.

For me, they were very loud—not like me at all. I had heard others speaking in soft tongues, but that's not how mine began, and then I knew it was of God because it was definitely not what I would choose for myself..

This is when the enemy steps in and says, "That's just you; you're making this all up." Do not believe him. Receive your gift! If you are having trouble, try asking God if something is blocking you.

I used to pray pretty prayers, but now my prayers seem clumsy. I stutter, repeat myself, and sometimes use a voice I don't even recognize, but they now carry all the authority of heaven. They are the most beautiful prayers I've ever heard. I value these strange prayers more than my flowery ones. This gift's main purpose is to enhance your personal prayer life and for praying God's heart.

The gift of prophecy is also useful in prayer. The Apostle Paul says to desire all the spiritual gifts, especially the gift of prophecy (1 Corinthians 14:1). When we speak what God reveals to us with a word, a vision, or a revelation, we are engaging in prophecy. Prophecy is not just foretelling (telling of what's to happen); it is also forth-telling. Forth-telling is declaring what God has revealed in order to bring it about. When we declare God's plan or forth-telling word, it releases the power of that word, and angels to carry out that word.

Praise the Lord, you angels, you mighty ones who carry out his plans, listening for each of his commands (Psalm 103:20 NLT).

Prophetic declaration releases breakthrough and destiny. When you pray prophetically over someone, you listen for God to say or show you something about that person, and then you speak it. When it is spoken, it releases the power to bring it about in that person's life. You may be speaking breakthrough for something they have been struggling with, breaking off things that have hindered them previously. This does not come from your own opinions or judgments, but from God and what He wants to do in their life.

You might speak about their destiny as well, revealing who they are and God's plans for them. According to Kris Vallotton in his book, *Basic Training for the Prophetic Ministry,* God shows you the "gold" inside them. He reveals the gold He means to bring forth and the potential they didn't know they had, so they can walk in that potential. Sometimes the person receives a new reality. What an awesome way to partner with God for what He wants to do in the lives of others!

Prophetic prayer has been instrumental in releasing things in me that God wants to do through my life. Recently, someone prophesied that I would write a book, and then that word began to manifest itself. You are now reading the product of that prophetic word.

I'll never forget the first time someone prayed prophetically over me. She told me how God saw me. She told me the private thoughts of God toward me. She used words only God and I would know. They meant something to me, because He had revealed the same things in prayer, but this woman couldn't have possibly have known that.

After she prayed things I already knew, she revealed things I didn't know, speaking words that released fire and passion that would set me on the path to my destiny. Not a destiny of my making, but God's destiny for me.

Spiritual gifts are for the benefit of others, to help them (1 Corinthians 12:7 NLT). Do not shy away from spiritual gifts, because they're essential for praying God's heart. Do not fear these supernatural gifts but embrace them and seek them out. Receive revelation and record it for the appointed time to deliver it.

> *I will stand on my guard post and station myself on the rampart; and I will keep watch to see what He will speak to me, and how I may reply when I am reproved. Then the Lord answered me and said, "Record the vision and inscribe it on tablets, that the one who reads it may run. For the vision I set for the appointed time; it hastens toward the goal, and it will not fail. Though it tarries, wait for it; for it will certainly come, it will not delay"* (Habakkuk 2:1-3 NASB)

The Censer

In Layer Four, we are a living censer, carrying the prayers of God's own heart. The Holy Spirit Himself ignites the incense. Our hearts blaze with the urgency of impassioned prayer that can find its release only by prevailing and travailing. The burden of the Lord becomes our anointed intercession as we enter into a divine power of agreement to release God's mercy. These are the prayers that tip the bowls (Revelation 5:8). Oh, the power this type of pure prayer must carry—persistence that accumulates power until the bowls tip. We are to be this living censer that receives God's fire to bring about God's plans on the earth.

> *Then another angel with a gold incense burner came and stood at the altar. And a great amount of incense was given to him to mix with the prayers of God's people as an offering on the gold alter before the throne. The smoke of the incense, mixed with the prayers of God's holy people ascended up to God from the altar where the angel had poured them out. Then the angel filled the incense burner with the fire from the altar and threw it down upon the earth; and thunder crashed, lightning flashed, and there was a terrible earthquake* (Revelation 8:3-5 NLT).

How should our prayers look in this layer? By this time, we should be at rest concerning cares as we fully trust in God's ability, faithfulness, and sovereignty. We're secure in our identity, and our only desire is the Holy Spirit. Our only thought is to praise Him and tell Him how much we love Him. We want only Him. Nothing else will satisfy. We are so deep in the well, we enter into His presence quickly and let Him love us as we love Him. This is the whole point of prayer.

Then we ask Him to bring us higher and reveal His message, His plan, and His heart so we can immediately begin to prevail for it. We pray only as we are led to pray, completely by the power of the Holy Spirit. We activate our spiritual gifts of tongues and prophecy in complete surrender to His leading. God knows what is needed. In this layer, we don't need to remind Him. He reminds us.

≈ *Fifteen* ≈

WALL: WARRING ANGELS AND LORD OF HEAVEN'S ARMIES

For He will command His angels concerning you to guard you in all your ways; they will lift you up in their hands, so that you will not strike your foot against a stone (Psalm 91:11-12 NLT).

Angels are involved in God's work on the earth. One function of angels is to guard us. The angel of the Lord is a guard; he surrounds and defends all who fear God (Psalm 34:7 NLT). They encircle the life of a believer. These angels are here to protect and assist us, and they're at our disposal. They wait to be activated. Angels are waiting for us to put them in the game, to give them a job to do.

In Genesis 28:10-22 (CSB), Jacob had a dream in which he saw angels ascending and descending from heaven. What are these angels doing? They come down from heaven with an assignment and ascend back up to heaven when they've completed their assignment.

God gives revelation to His people in dreams, and when Jacob awoke, he immediately realized he had received truth.

The angel delivered a message to Jacob, telling him who he was, and then he reminded Jacob of a promise God had made to his grandfather, Abraham.

Jacob also received a glimpse into the revelation of angelic activity. He named his resting place Bethel, meaning house of God. "What an awesome place this is! It is none other than the house of God, the very gateway to heaven!" (Genesis 28:17)

A gateway is an opening something can pass through. We live under an open heaven, where angels come and go, on assignment from God and activated by us. If we need protection, we can activate our warring angels because they wage war on our behalf. In the battle of good vs. evil or right vs. wrong, angels will always hold up God's standard because God is the "Lord of Heaven's Armies." This name (or sometimes Lord of Hosts) is used more than 250 times in the Old Testament. This is the name we want to call on in order to activate the angels who are here to help us.

If you are weak or need help, you can activate your ministering angels. "Are not all angels ministering spirits sent to serve those who will inherit salvation?" (Hebrews 1:14). Angels ministered to Jesus when He was in the wilderness for forty days and forty nights (Matthew 4:11 ESV). He had just resisted the devil's third temptation, and angels came to minister to Him. We can expect God to send angels to minister to us as well, in our time of need because His word says, "He sends His angels like the winds, his servants like flames of fire." (Hebrews 1:7 NLT) Not only does He send His angels, but He rides on their wings into your situation. Look what the Psalms have to say about this.

He makes the clouds His chariot and rides on the wings of the wind. He makes winds his messengers, flames of fire his servants (Psalm 104:3-4).

He rode upon the cherub and flew, and He sped upon the wings of the wind (Psalm 18:10).

When you call upon the Lord of Heaven's Armies, He rides in on the angels He dispatches. Picture it! You are not putting your faith in angels but in the One who sends them and rides on their wings.

Angels intervene in our daily lives, and they are at our service to assist us with God's purposes. But we must learn to activate them. We can call on angels to minister to our personal needs as well as those of our family, our church, and even those we pray for. As Joshua Mills states in his book *Moving in Glory Realms*, "Under the old covenant, the people of God didn't have authority to command angels. Today, angels wait for our command because we have been given authority over them in the name of Jesus."

Now Christ has gone to heaven. He is seated in the place of honor next to God, and all the angels and authorities and powers accept his authority (1 Peter 3:22 NLT).

And Christ has given us authority. The Bible also says, "Don't you realize that we believers will judge angels?" (1 Corinthians 6:3). We cannot judge something unless we have authority over them.

Obedience is the key to activating your angels. Live your life in obedience to the Father, keeping Him as your first love, spending time in His presence, worshipping with songs of praises, and speaking the Scriptures. Choosing this lifestyle liberates our angels to get involved in our lives.

You may not see your angels or feel their presence, but they are all around, curious about what you are doing and talking about. Here's a hint: if you are always talking about God, they want to be near you to listen in. If you listen to worship music, they want to join in the singing. This is the activity they are attracted to.

Begin to look around your house. You may see evidence of your angels. My daughter and I periodically find tiny white feathers lying in the oddest places, like our bathroom countertop. I keep them to remind myself that my angels are there, standing guard and ready for service. I sometimes catch my cat staring at something either above my head or on the ceiling. I can't help but think she sees my angel.

Sometimes we need to rest, knowing the battle belongs to the Lord. Many times He fights our battles for us (2 Chronicles 32:8 NLT). He goes before us, and when He does, the battle is won. As we see in 2 Chronicles 20, the Moabites, Ammonites, and some of the Meunites declared war on King Jehoshaphat. Terrified, Jehoshaphat begged the Lord for guidance. Sometimes we need God to show us what to do, but other times, God simply says, "Stand still. I've got this."

The Bible tells us the Spirit of the Lord came upon one of the men standing around, and he began to speak a message from the Lord. Isn't this exciting? God can come upon you at any time to deliver an important message, and it might be just what someone needs to hear. Listen to what the man says:

Listen, all you people of Judah and Jerusalem! Listen, King Jehoshaphat! This is what the Lord says: Do not be afraid! Don't be discouraged by this mighty army, for the battle is not yours, but God's . . . You will not even need to fight. Take your positions; then stand still and watch the Lord's victory (2 Chronicles 20:15-17 NLT).

The king told the people to believe in the Lord their God, and then they could stand firm. The people began to sing and praise the Lord, and their singing and praising caused the armies to fight among themselves.

Worship is a weapon. Whenever and wherever God's people praise Him, He reigns among them and does miraculous things on their behalf. We don't have to do a thing except believe and stand firm. By so doing, we steward a "glory bubble."

In righteousness you will be established; you will be far from oppression, for you will not fear; and from terror, for it will not come near you (Isaiah 54:14 ESV).

There is a place where you can be so established that terrors will not even be allowed to come near you, and that place is inside the glory bubble where nothing is impossible with God!

I was once at a conference and heard Mahesh Chavda speak about this glory bubble. He said, "As we receive more from God, an energy and dynamic comes over us; a type of shield like a 'dome of glory,' where nothing can harm us." Weeks later, I was on the highway, and I looked in my rearview mirror to see a car speeding in the right lane to get between me and the car behind me. There was no room for him to get over, but he tried to cut in anyway. He moved into the left lane and clipped the front end of the car behind me. They both spun and veered off into the ditch like two colliding race cars. All this happened just feet from the back end of my van. Protected in my glory bubble, I was untouched and unharmed. All I had to do was be still and stay in my lane.

When we operate in the glory, heaven's armies protect us. Where there is glory, there are angels, and where there are angels, there is glory (Matthew 25:31 BLB). You can't separate them.

Thoughts on Layer Four

When you're in the rivers, you're in the glory. You operate under an open heaven, and you have access to angels. You receive revelation from God, using all the spiritual gifts within the fullness of the Holy Spirit. He guides all your prayers and brings you into spontaneous worship of a loving Father, no matter where you are. This is the place meant for every born-again, Spirit-filled believer. Does it seem too incredible? Too unbelievable? Too marvelous?

No eye has seen, no ear has heard, no heart has imagined, what God has prepared for those who love Him (1 Corinthians 2:9 NLT).

How badly do you want it? It is an endless pursuit, total commitment. God is not only desiring to be believed, but He is waiting to be experienced. These encounters are life-changing for those who'd dare to dive into the well. Is there more beyond Layer Four? Are there deeper layers? I believe the answer is yes! There is always more to God. I believe there is no end to the depths. You cannot go beyond God because He is the one who is beyond. If I discover deeper layers, I will write a sequel to this book and tell you all about it. That is, unless you get there first, then you can tell me.

For now we see only a reflection as in a mirror; then we shall see face to face. Now I know in part; then I shall know fully, even as I am fully known (1 Corinthians 13:12).

Discussion Questions

1. How has the filling or the baptism of the Holy Spirit become clearer to you as you travel through the layers? Can you describe the difference between water baptism and the baptism of the Holy Spirit? What is the purpose of each?

2. What is the difference between natural senses and spiritual senses? How does that relate to sight and hearing, since they are considered both?

3. What are spiritual gifts? How do they relate to the idea that God wants to display Himself through us?

4. What does it mean to go higher? What do you want to receive?

5. How do you feel about the gift of speaking in tongues? Why is the gift of tongues essential for your personal prayer time and to prevailing in prayer?

6. What are the benefits of the gift of prophecy? How can we use it in personal prayer and prayer for others?

7. How are angels involved in our lives? How can we activate them? Why should we?

8. What do you identify with most in this layer? What do you still struggle to understand?

Final Thoughts

≈ Sixteen ≈

UNIVERSAL JOURNEY

Our personal journey—how we come to Jesus—is unique to us. Our stories vary from one person to the next. We are all scattered across this earth, but God is gathering His flock. Like a good shepherd, He comes to find each one of us (Matthew 18:12). He wants to bring us all home, where we belong. Once we're found, once we're gathered, our journey connects us to a journey as old as time itself.

Once upon a time, there was a people living in a great place. Life was good until it got harder and harder. It wasn't long before these people began to feel like slaves. The promise of a good life somewhere along the line had been broken. It happened slowly over time, but the people were chained to this once-great place, in bondage to things they never meant to be slaves to. They asked themselves, "When did this started happening and when did it become our lifestyle?"

One day a man came along and told them strange things. "This is not who you are. You are not supposed to be slaves. You're a chosen people. Come with me, and I will take you out of this place."

They liked what he was saying, but they were scared. However, they decided to trust him. So the man went to the slave master and said, "Let my people go! I want to take them away from here so they can worship God." After much interceding on their behalf, the slave master finally agreed, and they left what they had known for so long to follow a man who'd promised them freedom, a place flowing with milk and honey, streets paved with gold, and an end to their sorrow and pain.

They turned from that life and followed the promise. But the slave master changed his mind and pursued them. The old life chased them until they came to a place where they felt trapped. Should they go back?

But the man said, "Trust me. Come this way, right through the water."

They made their decision and went through the water. As they did, their enemy followed them but the water soon swallowed him up. They came out on the other side, free! The old life was gone, along with all it represented. They were washed by that water, redeemed by that water, saved by that water. This was the first day of their new life.

Even though they were no longer captives, they didn't know how to worship God as the man wanted them to. So, instead of taking them straight to the place he'd promised, he took them on a longer journey to teach them. God went with them. He was always there in front of them and behind them. But the journey was long and unfamiliar, so they began to complain and long for the life they had left behind.

Now that they thought about it, that life seemed easier. They wanted to worship their familiar gods. Even though God had saved them, they couldn't see Him as their one true

God. He was not enough. They wanted their idols too.

So, the man brought them to a mountain to show the people God, high and lifted up, mighty and powerful. They saw lightning coming from the mountaintop. He was like a mighty King sitting on a powerful throne. Once they saw Him for who He was, they began to try to follow His laws. The man taught them God's ways, and he gave them new identities and new jobs to do. Now they went about their days trusting God, learning how to worship and serve Him.

One day God brought them to their promised location. The day had finally come, but they were still untrusting. They decided to send some ahead to take a look, because surely they knew better than God if this was the place for them. Still relying on their own understanding, not fully realizing who they were or who was with them, they decided not to claim the promise. They were scared of what they would face. They were not confident in their abilities. They didn't believe the promises, and they didn't think they had authority to take this promise for themselves.

They went back into the desert for more time to learn, to circle the same mountain a few more times. Over and over, they encountered the same obstacles, got a glimpse of the promise, but they weren't allowed to go in until the day they understood who they were. They were chosen to claim this promise, and God was with them to do the hard work. He had promised it, so it must already be theirs. They just had to claim it. The man said, "Yes, it is yours. Go claim it. But I cannot go with you. I will give you another leader who will be with you."

So they came to another river. This river flowed before them and their promise. They decided to dedicate themselves wholly to their God. They went through the river, but this time God did not merely watch from the other side. He went through the river with them.

They all passed a second time in the water, and they came through to the other side with power to take that promise. But first they had to take down a mighty walled city, inhabited by a new enemy.

They were a new people, filled with power they didn't have before. They marched against that city with God going before them. They marched and sang and shouted with all their might, and the walls crumbled. The victory was won! A people who were once slaves now walked in power with a great inheritance.

Did you recognize the story? You may see it as the story of Moses leading the Israelites out of Egypt. Or you might see it as your story—the story of being born again and Jesus leading you home. In either case, you would be right. It's the same story. A universal journey. A journey of crossing over from one life to another. A journey that must happen in the life of every believer if they want to see the Kingdom of God.

I tell you the truth, unless you are born again, you cannot see the Kingdom of God (John 3:3 NLT).

Being born again simply means crossing over from an old life to a new life, leaving one realm (darkness), and entering a new realm (light). It's crossing over from one land of captivity and slavery to a new land of promise. Jesus is the King of Crossing Over as He has crossed the ultimate barrier from death to life. When we make Him our King, we are born again and have crossed over into this life. Our personal journey through the well is us learning how to live in that crossed over life, a life in the Spirit. Our first birth was that of the the natural, but our second birth is that of the Spirit. We don't know how to live in the Spirit, so we need to learn, just as Jesus had to learn to live in the natural when He left heaven as a spiritual being to become a man. He showed us how to be both, and we must learn how to be both. Through the layers, God teaches us how to walk, see, feel, and hear in the Spirit in order to live as a spiritual being while being human.

Did you see the layers within the story? Go back and identify them. The Bible is full of stories that contain the layers. Why? Because they are a divine order. It is the order God has put in place to bring us out of captivity and bondage and into power and promise. This order cannot happen without God's presence. Notice that God was always with the people, guiding them and teaching them. God does not let you go through the layers without Him. In fact, we cannot do it alone. The divine order is designed to take you deeper into His presence, gaining greater knowledge of Him, yourself, and your purpose.

I recognized the layers in Pastor Dale Everett's sermon "The Path of More." Teaching from 2 Kings 2:1-15 as his text, it's the story of the prophet Elijah and his apprentice, Elisha. Elijah is about to take a journey, right before he was to be taken up to heaven. Elisha knew this, and he wanted to join him on this journey. He wasn't going to leave him or let him out of his sight, so he accompanied Elijah.

He was concerned about his mentor, but more than that, he was after something. He wanted the "more." He was so hungry for it, he dedicated himself to this journey, so when the time was right, he would receive what Elijah had. How closely are you willing to follow the Master in order to get what He has for you?

They started their journey at Gilgal. Each place on Elijah and Elisha's journey had special significance. Gilgal represents a place of separation. It was at Gilgal that the Israelites stopped to be circumcised in order to consecrate themselves to the Lord before they entered the Promised Land. This was an act of separating themselves for God's purpose as a type of sanctification. Sanctification or separation for God requires sacrifice. You must be willing to lay everything down or you won't get to the next step on the journey. There is no success without sacrifice.

How do you lay things down? You start by emptying, not gathering. Stop gathering and start emptying. The starting point for Elisha was Layer One, as it is for us.

The first place they came to was Bethel, which represents the house of God. This is where God shows up on your journey. You think this is it, and you want to stay there forever. It's a revelatory place, much like Layer Two—a place of worship. Pastor Everett says, "The level of worship will always be in the dimension of the revelation or level of how God revealed Himself to you."

You may be tempted to stop here, because you're in a good place. In fact, Elijah told Elisha not to go any farther with him. He should stay right here.

But Elisha is after more. He travels with him to Jericho, the walled city. Jericho represents a place of battle, a place of testing. It is important to know this when you are in this place. Resist discouragement, thinking you're in the wrong place. You may feel that way in Layer Three, but being in a battle doesn't necessarily mean you've gotten off the path or taken a detour from the journey. No, quite the opposite. This is where you put on your armor and do everything to stand. Great victories will come out of great battles!

Again, Elijah asks Elisha to stay. You might also get caught up in the battle and think that is where you should stay, fighting for yourself, fighting for your family, or fighting for causes. But Elisha still had his eye on more, and so should you.

Then they come to the Jordan (the second river from my story). The Jordan represents the place of no return. Once you've crossed over, you're changed. You have full commitment. Just as in Layer Four, this river takes you from purpose to promise.

Also, it takes a miracle to get through. Elijah struck the water with his cloak, dividing it so they could cross. Elisha saw this miracle and knew what was possible for him, but he had to ask for it. In essence, he said, "I want a double portion of what you have." That's a big request. But it's what Jesus says we should want: to do what He did and even greater things.

At that moment, God took Elijah to heaven in a whirlwind, and Elisha was left much like the disciples were when Jesus ascended to heaven. He had a promise and an assignment. What was he going to do with it? He went back to the Jordan River and did exactly what Elijah had done. He struck the water and said, "Where is the Lord, the God of Elijah?" Then the river divided and Elisha went across, and all who watched knew that the Spirit now rested upon Elisha.

When we step into that river, God will show up for us and will rest upon us, and everyone who watches our journey will know it. They will see us go from captive to bride. As captives we are tied—to our sins, idols, and the lies of the enemy. From there we become servants. He will teach and train us, but He wants us to be His friend. As a friend, we trust Him with our lives. He trusts us with His mysteries. Ultimately, we become the bride, and He takes the bride. He takes us to heights that we can't achieve on our own. In the end, He's coming back to take His bride.

Let us rejoice and be glad and give Him glory! For the wedding of the Lamb has come, and His bride has made herself ready (Revelation 19:7).

Are you a ready bride? You don't want to miss "the time of your visitation" (Luke 19:44). Jesus was with humanity for thirty-three years and ministered for the last three years of His life. Yet, when He approached Jerusalem right before His last Passover, the Bible says He wept over Jerusalem. Why did He weep? It wasn't because He knew His time was drawing near, or because He would suffer. No, it was because He had been with them all this time, and they had missed it. Luke 19:44 quotes Jesus at that moment.

You did not know the time of your visitation (ESV).

You did not recognize the time of God's coming to you.

You did not recognize it when God visited you (NLT).

How did they miss their visitation, and how can we avoid missing our visitation? Let's not fall into the same pitfalls. Bethlehem didn't make room for Him (Luke 2:7), and so they missed the time of their visitation. Nazareth couldn't change their perspective of Him (Luke 4:22, 28-29), and so they missed the time of their visitation. Martha in Bethany was too busy and distracted with many things (Luke 10:40-41), and so she missed the time of her visitation. Judas wouldn't allow Jesus to change him (Luke 22:3-6), and so he missed the time of his visitation. And finally, Jerusalem wouldn't adjust their expectations of Him, and so they missed the time of their visitation.

I almost missed the time of my visitation when I recently visited Jerusalem. I went there with high expectations of how God would touch me and how I would encounter Him. As the days went by and the specific things I expected didn't happen, I began to get discouraged. But His glory was all around me, and I could feel it physically. The problem was, I didn't recognize it because I was too caught up in my own expectations.

We need to give up our expectation of what He will do in our lives. He may use you differently than how He uses me, and your encounters may be completely different than mine. Be like a garden through which He can walk freely (as in the time of Adam and Eve), tilling soil, planting seeds where He sees fit, pruning areas He wants to prune, and sending rain when He determines the time is right. Present yourself as an empty garden and allow Him to cultivate and bring you to life. Remember, you are an empty vessel, dead to self.

Because you have died to self, the only thing left is Christ in you. You have the incarnation of Christ (the Holy Spirit) living inside you. Dr. Clarice Fluitt says it like this, "Christ in you is the hope of glory, but Christ as you is the manifestation." When you act as Christ did, He can manifest (express Himself) through you. Notice it is not you. It is Christ in you as you.

If this isn't a big enough revelation of who you are, let me tell you another secret about your identity. God's name for Himself is "I Am." Did you know that every time you speak of who you are, you can't help but say the name of God first? I am Kim. It's like a title. Who God is precedes who I am. Every time I claim who I am, I first acknowledge God. I belong to Him. If I start my name with Mrs., everyone knows I belong to someone. When I say, "I am Kim," it says I belong to God. Now say, "I am Christ in me." You are who God says you are. Now go, be Christ as you.

Final Thoughts

He will baptize you with the Holy Spirit and fire (Matthew 3:11).

Did you notice that you are the censer in every layer? What is the censer filled with? Fire. When He puts His fire in us, we become a torch, a fire carrier. On the day of Pentecost, tongues of fire rested on the heads of each of the 120 who were in the room, setting them ablaze with the Holy Spirit and fire. When the fire came, it separated into flames and landed on 120 different heads. Ultimately, these 120 torches were responsible for 3,000 people being saved that day. No faithful believer who waited in that room was left out.

If we wait faithfully, the fire will fall on us. We will not be left out. In fact, that flame of fire will fuel our assignment. This flame burning inside us cannot be contained. And when we get close to others, the fire we carry can spread to them. We can be so contagious for God that others feel our fire and want what we have. We can light a fire within someone else.

God calls each of us to be a torch bearer, carrying His light and fire into dark and cold places.

Many Christians don't know they should look for this fire. They don't even know this fire is out there. Will you be the one to receive it, to house His fire? Will you be the one God uses to release it? Will you be the one to ignite someone else's torch? Will you carry the fire? Will you be the one?

I pray in the name of Jesus that the fire I carry will leap from these pages and land on you. Be so filled with the fire of His passion that you begin to carry that flame. I release an impartation of fire now.

A Promise of Restoration and Inheritance

In that day I will restore the fallen house of David. I will repair its damaged walls. From the ruins I will rebuild it and restore its former glory (Amos 9:11 NLT).

Then I saw a new heaven and a new earth, for the old heaven and the old earth had disappeared. And the sea was also gone. And I saw the holy city, the new Jerusalem, coming down from God out of heaven like a bride beautifully dressed for her husband.

I heard a loud shout from the throne, saying, "Look, God's home is now among his people! He will live with them, and they will be his people. God himself will be with them. He will wipe every tear from their eyes, and there will be no more death or sorrow or crying or pain. All these things are gone forever."

And the one sitting on the throne said, "Look, I am making everything new!" And then he said to me, "Write this down, for what I tell you is trustworthy and true."

And he also said, "It is finished! I am the Alpha and the Omega—the Beginning and the End. To all who are thirsty I will give freely from the springs of the water of life. All who are victorious will inherit all these blessings, and I will be their God, and they will be my children" (Revelation 21:1-7 NLT).

The Spirit and the bride say, "Come." Let anyone who hears this say, "Come." Let anyone who is thirsty come. Let anyone who desires, drink freely from the water of life (Revelation 22:17 NLT).

Prayer for Salvation

Have you made Jesus Lord of your life and rightful King in your heart? Do you want to cross over into the new life and become a new creation, secure in your identity and authority? Do you want to partner with the Holy Spirit and receive the freedom and promise that is your inheritance? If you answered yes, then pray this prayer and believe in your heart:

Father, I confess that I have not put You in Your rightful place in my heart or in my life. I am a sinner in captivity, enslaved by the power of these sins. Please forgive me. Today I make a decision to make You Lord of my life and King of my heart. I surrender all idols and submit to You. Come and give me the Holy Spirit that I may turn from my sin and begin a new journey, following You. I want to cross over and become a new creation. Help me to become an empty vessel so You can fill me with Your love and tell me who I am in You. Show me Your purposes for my life. Fill me with Your fire, so my heart will burn more passionately for You and bring me more and more into an intimate relationship with You in Your presence. Help me to know You more and experience You more. Bring my life into a divine order that leads to more encounters with You. I want to come to You thirsty. Bring me deep into Your well. Only You can make this transformation, and I give You permission to bring me out of the darkness and into Your glorious light. By the power of the Holy Spirt and in the mighty name of Jesus, amen.

One thing I ask from the Lord, this only do I seek: that I may dwell in the house of the Lord all the days of my life, to gaze on the beauty of the Lord and to seek Him in his temple (Psalm 27:4).

About the Author

Kim Patterson is a wife and mother of three. She has been a leader in her church for the past 13 years, leading various small groups and teaching Bible studies. Kim has a passion for women's ministries and discipleship. It is her love for the Lord that fuels her desire to see others grow in Christ and walk in freedom and victory. Kim is a recent graduate from the JFA School of Supernatural Ministry (Bethel Curriculm).

For more information, visit the author's website at:
www.tothethirsty.com